Teach® Yourself

Get Started in Writing a Novel

Nigel Watts and Stephen May

with additional material by
Jodie Daber

First published in Great Britain in 2012 by Hodder & Stoughton. An Hachette UK company.

First published in US in 2012 by The McGraw-Hill Companies, Inc.

Previously published as *How to Write a Novel and Get it Published*

This updated and expanded edition published 2015

British Library Cataloguing in Publication Data: a catalogue record for this title is available from the British Library.

Library of Congress Catalog Card Number: on file.

Paperback ISBN 978 1 473 611696

ebook ISBN 978 1 473 611702

1

The publisher has used its best endeavours to ensure that any website addresses referred to in this book are correct and active at the time of going to press. However, the publisher and the author have no responsibility for the websites and can make no guarantee that a site will remain live or that the content will remain relevant, decent or appropriate.

The publisher has made every effort to mark as such all words which it believes to be trademarks. The publisher should also like to make it clear that the presence of a word in the book, whether marked or unmarked, in no way affects its legal status as a trademark.

Every reasonable effort has been made by the publisher to trace the copyright holders of material in this book. Any errors or omissions should be notified in writing to the publisher, who will endeavour to rectify the situation for any reprints and future editions.

Typeset by Cenveo® Publisher Services.

Printed and bound in Great Britain by CPI Group (UK) Ltd., Croydon, CR0 4YY.

John Murray Learning policy is to use papers that are natural, renewable and recyclable products and made from wood grown in sustainable forests. The logging and manufacturing processes are expected to conform to the environmental regulations of the country of origin.

John Murray Learning
Carmelite House
50 Victoria Embankment
London EC4Y 0DZ

Also available in ebook

Contents

Introduction

There are only three rules to writing a successful novel. Unfortunately, nobody knows what the three rules are.

Perhaps only another novelist would see the joke, but it's worth telling, because, as with most jokes, there is wisdom tucked inside it. If you strip away the details of a successful novel, you are left with something very simple, and it is easy to believe there is a three-step plan to reproducing a successful novel for yourself. Take character 'X', put him in situation 'Y', and make event 'Z' happen to him – lo and behold, instant success, fame, money. If it was that easy, of course, we would all be millionaires. But it isn't that easy – in fact, the closer you look, the less easy it appears. Why? Just because something is simple, it doesn't mean it's not mysterious. A novel is simple, just as a flower is simple, but try making one for yourself. We can't – all we can do is to help one grow. We can plant a seed of thought, water it with attention and then we just have to wait. The word 'author' is from the Latin *auctor*, which literally means 'one who makes to grow'. Though we can try to build novels in the way a child builds a sandcastle, at the heart of a successful novel is a mysterious and indefinable 'author-ing', an organic growing of a story. The reason nobody knows the three rules to writing a successful novel is that if there *are* three rules, they are unknowable.

The apprenticeship of writing

Whoever said that writing can't be taught, only learned, was on to something. What does the expression mean? It means that although writing requires an apprenticeship, it is an apprenticeship whose duration is internal rather than simply a matter of turning up to class. Nobody can teach another person something as complex as writing a novel. The most a teacher can do is to point out the way, make suggestions, indicate the pitfalls and hold a mirror up to the students so they can learn for themselves. And although success is attainable from the very beginning, there is no end to the apprenticeship. A good writer will always be a student of writing.

Rabindranath Tagore, the great Indian poet, was visited on his deathbed by an eminent critic and friend. 'You have much of which to be proud,' the friend said. 'Six thousand poems you have written, each one a masterpiece. You can die content in the knowledge that you have been a flower which has fully opened.'

Rabindranath began to weep, much to the astonishment of the critic. 'Why are you weeping, my friend? Does death frighten you so?'

'I am not afraid of death. I am weeping because I have only just become a poet. Up to now my buds have only been half open. More and more poems are coming to me, each one better than the last. I am weeping at the injustice of being so quickly pruned by God.'

There is no end to the journey towards the perfect poem or the perfect novel. Why? Because no such thing exists. If you find yourself writing and rewriting a sentence, groping towards a perfect expression of what you want to say, do yourself a favour – stop it. Not only can there never be a perfect novel, there cannot even be a perfect sentence. Words are symbols: the best they can do is approximate what we want to say. And just as what we want to say is, hopefully, ever expanding, so too is our ability to use words which fit.

You can learn the craft of writing, but the teacher is yourself. A book such as this one can be invaluable – use it, take heed by all means; however, the lessons will be learned when you are holding a pen in your hand, and you can become your own instructor.

Art and craft

Another way of expressing this idea is: *You can teach craft, but art can only be learned.* A novel, as any piece of creative writing, comprises two aspects: the craft, that is, the *mechanics* of its construction, and the art, namely the *quality* of its construction. The mechanics of writing can easily be learned: a page of diagrams can be memorized, a list digested – and you will find both in this book. Quality, however, is more difficult to learn, for it can't be reduced to a formula. Quality is the indefinable mystery of writing, the relationship between words, which is as much the product of the space between words as the words themselves. A mechanical approach to writing a novel will always fall short of what is possible for the form – we can use computer programs to help us with plot ideas and to check our grammar, but no computer can write a good novel, because no computer can understand this mystery.

A good writer isn't just a wordsmith. A good writer is someone who can see quality in the world and can somehow translate that on to the page. Tricky to achieve, but essential if we are to write a novel which touches people.

The myth of the 'writer'

If you are the sort of person to be intimidated by the weight of books that have already been written, or are unsure of your talent or your vocation, take heart. There is no such personage as a 'writer'. If you worry that you don't possess that special ingredient other writers have, particularly the writers you admire – don't. There is only one qualification to be a writer: human beingness.

Juan Carlos Onetti

'I am not a writer except when I write.'

It took me years before I could call myself a writer, years more before I realized the term means nothing. A writer is a person who writes. A novelist is a person who writes novels. And a good novelist? We're back to the mystery – there is no absolute checklist against which we can measure our writing. Anyone who has received enough feedback – whether from friends or from professional reviewers – knows that everyone has a different idea about what makes a good book, a good writer. If you want a lesson in the futility of measuring up to the notion 'good writer', just try to write something which pleases everybody. It is important to listen to people's opinions, particularly those who have trodden that path before; however, just as the essence of the perfect sentence is ineffable, so too is that quality marked 'excellence'. Why else do some novelists write again and again and again? Not for the money, nor the limelight, nor even because they have a story burning a hole in their mind, but because they are reaching for a distant star, just as Tagore was.

Do I have what it takes?

Leaving aside notions of good and bad, what sort of person writes, in particular a novel? If you wonder whether you have the stamina to complete a novel or the talent to write a good one, there is only one way to find out – write one and see. If you wonder whether the journey is worth the effort, whether you stand any chance of reaching the end, there are some questions you could ask yourself before you start. Do I enjoy reading? Have I turned to pen and paper in times of turmoil? Am I interested in people, and what makes them tick? Do I have a story to tell, or a message I want people to hear? Have I ever been complimented on my writing?

Although there is no such person as a writer, and although people who write are as various as the books that have been written, I imagine most people who have written successful novels would answer 'yes' to most of the above questions.

The importance of being a reader

If you were an avid reader as a child, all well and good (though don't rule yourself out if this is not the case – some of us come to books only later in life). Nevertheless, it is important that you read a certain amount now. This is for two reasons: first, whether you are avant-garde or a genre writer, self-consciously literary or don't know how to define yourself as a writer, you must realize that your work, if read, will be gauged by people who are expert story consumers. Even if your readers haven't read widely, it is likely they have read a bit. And what about the plays or films your readers have seen? We are the most story-literate society ever – stories are everywhere, and not just in obvious forms. Stories are disguised as news reports and adverts; jokes are nothing but funny stories, gossip nothing but domestic stories. We are experts on our own culture – and although we may not be able to tell a good story, we know one when we hear one. So, if you want to please such discriminating consumers, you need to realize you are part of a cultural tradition. That doesn't mean you have to read all the classics; it does mean you can't be completely uninformed. It is no good thinking you are being startlingly original if everyone else thinks it's old hat. It's no good unwittingly conforming to genre and then unwittingly switching in mid-story – readers will accuse you of cheating, just as if you had picked up the ball in a game of soccer.

The second reason you should be a reader is to learn from others. Apprentices work under craftspeople so they can study their technique, and novel writing requires an apprenticeship just as much as furniture making. At first you may find yourself copying other writers, certainly, this was so in my case: my first novel began as a pastiche of many different styles – from Jane Austen to D. H. Lawrence to Kurt Vonnegut. Thankfully, I managed to break free of their influence, but at first it may not have been a bad thing: there is much to learn in terms of syntax and rhythm and authority from all three writers. In the end, however, it is vital that you find your own voice. If not, the story will just be a thinly veiled copy of a better original, whether that be Tom Clancy or Tom Stoppard. Learn from other writers, and by all means (the laws of copyright withstanding) borrow from them, but make your words your own.

T. S. Eliot

'A poor poet imitates, a good poet steals.'

Three qualities needed for success

There are three qualities I think an aspiring writer needs in order to have success: luck, talent and hard work. There may not be much you can do about luck (although what some people call good luck in others is often the legitimate fruit of their labours). Talent – the ability to mould quality – you can do more about, although you can only develop something that is already there. It is hard work which is most fully available to us. Writing well is not a doddle. Yes, sometimes the muse descends on us, and all we have to do is hold the pen. Most of the time, however, it involves struggle and discomfort. If novelists wrote only when they were inspired, the shelves of our libraries would be mostly empty.

THE IMPORTANCE OF STAMINA

Writing a novel, more so than writing a short story or a poem, requires *stamina*. When I began my first novel, I leaped into it as though I was running a 100-yard dash. A few days passed, a few weeks, and I found myself pausing to catch my breath, looking ahead to see where the finishing line lay. It was nowhere in sight – I had barely finished the first chapter. A novel, I realized, is not a dash, but a marathon. A few weeks passed, a few months, and I realized my metaphor was wrong – a marathon, even at walking pace, can be completed in a day. Perhaps the writing of a novel was closer to an extended pregnancy. A few months passed, turning into a few years, and I realized that, again, I had got the wrong image. Bar any mishaps, there is something inevitable about pregnancy. If you allow nature to take its course, there is no turning back: a baby will be born. There is no such certainty for a novel. You could work on a novel for ever without coming to its end – there is nothing inevitable about completing it.

COURAGE AND ENCOURAGEMENT

As well as stamina, you also need something which may not be immediately apparent, particularly at the start – *courage*. Why does writing take courage? Nobody is going to write your novel for you, and it won't write itself. The only way a novel will be written is by you picking up the pen and writing every word – a writer, remember, is someone who writes, not someone who thinks about writing. When the going gets tough, and your story is in a tight corner, or your characters have turned to cardboard, and your enthusiasm to sawdust, there is only one person who can pull you though – yourself. Disciplining yourself to work when you don't want to, climbing back into the saddle when your story throws you, believing in yourself when nobody else does – these things take courage. It is far easier not to write a novel than it is to write one. Writers need every little bit of encouragement they can get. So, before you start your project, or if you're in the middle of it, pause for a moment, reach over your shoulder and pat yourself on the back. Even if you're only contemplating writing a novel, congratulate yourself. There are far more people who would like to have written a novel than who want to write, far more people who want to write than actually do so. Encourage yourself regularly in the writing – or better still, find someone who can offer encouragement to you, and you will find that you are a writer.

CLIMBING THE LITERARY MOUNTAIN

Of the three qualities of luck, talent and hard work, it is the last with which you should make friends. The successful novelist (that is, one who has finished a project which is recognizably a novel) is a stubborn, brave and single-minded individual. Antisocial, perhaps; misunderstood, almost certainly; confused and afraid at times, unsure of their talent, regretful of their mistakes, envious of their peers – a successful novelist may be all of these. But he or she is also a brave pioneer.

It will help make the journey less onerous if you remind yourself occasionally why you want to write. The two essential qualities every novelist needs – motivation and inspiration – are contrary creatures which rebel against coercion. You must coax them, encouraging them, promising them that the journey is worth the effort. Convince yourself that for the person who reaches the top of his or her literary Everest and plants the flag, there is immense satisfaction. If you have yet to make such a journey, just know that the view from the top of a completed novel is, in my experience, worth the struggle.

NO RULES

If you learn nothing else from the book, I would like you to learn this: THERE ARE NO RULES. A novel is not a wind-up machine which either works or it doesn't – it is a social convention which is constantly changing. Admittedly, some conventions are so embedded in our culture that we would be unwise to ignore them, just as we would be unwise to drive on the wrong side of the road. But fiction is not real life, and the cost of breaking with convention is often no more than failure to be published. This is part of the pleasure of writing fiction – the freedom from constraint.

If you do want to be published, following the advice in this book will probably help, because the majority of the points I make are a matter of consensus. However, slavishly following a convention is not only misguided, it can be unhelpful: a good novel is a strange thing – you can break every 'rule' in the book and still write a wonderful bestseller. In fact, the best novels are often those which take the biggest chances. It is worth realizing, however, that people who do this successfully are usually experts in the conventions they are breaking. Be well informed, and *then* fly in the face of tradition. Pablo Picasso only became a successful Cubist when he had already mastered classical drawing.

Some of my advice in the following pages is more idiosyncratic, in which case it is even further away from being a rule. But I cannot teach you the craft of writing, because no such craft exists: all I can do is try to teach you *my* craft of writing.

HOW TO USE THIS BOOK

I have structured this book to reflect my own process of writing a novel. Although fiction writing is far too messy to submit to such analysis, my journey goes something like this: I begin with the idea, develop the plot, find out who my characters are, then decide viewpoint, setting and theme. Editing comes way down the line, and the last thing I think about is selling the novel.

Obviously, some writers might perform this process in reverse, so there are two ways to use this book. First, by starting at page one and working your way through it; or second, by using it as a workshop manual, dipping in as you progress with your own novel. The Contents at the front (and the Index at the back, if you're reading the paperback version of this book) will help you find what you're looking for.

ABOUT THE EXERCISES

Throughout most of the chapters there are suggested exercises. If you choose to do them, a note of caution – don't turn them into a chore. If this happens, stop – it may become counter-productive. But distinguish between a deep-seated distaste for what you're doing and a temporary reluctance based on laziness or fear. If you meet a barrier, and want to stop, try pushing past it. Often, on the other side is what you've been looking for.

Here's your key to the different types of exercise and feature:

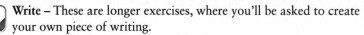

Write – These are longer exercises, where you'll be asked to create your own piece of writing.

Snapshot – A shorter exercise, or a series of questions to help you consider a particular aspect of the writing process.

Workshop – A series of guided questions that will help you reflect on a piece of writing – see below for a more detailed explanation.

Edit – A chance to rework and strengthen a piece you've already created.

Key quote – Words of wisdom from those who know.

Key idea – An important concept to grasp.

Focus point – Advice to take forward.

Next step – Where we're going next.

THE WORKSHOP

This edition of includes a brand-new exercise – the Workshop. Creative writing workshops provide writers of all abilities and from all backgrounds with a space in which to share their work and get constructive feedback. They are also great places to meet like-minded people and share the agonies and ecstasies of becoming a writer. There's probably one happening near you. Ask at your local library or adult education centre for details.

In the Workshop exercises, you'll get the chance to review your novel-in-progress. There'll be a series of questions which will hopefully help you to see the piece through new eyes, to identify what's successful and what isn't, and guide you towards ways to strengthen and hone your writing, just like attending a workshop in real life.

1

Beginnings

You want to write a novel, so where do you start? Let's first of all dismiss the topic of technology. A computer is helpful: it makes editing easy, likewise printing out copies. Some people find that having, in effect, a neat top copy always in front of their eyes helps them keep their thoughts ordered. A spell checker and word counter are also helpful features.

On a humbler level, paper and pen or pencil have been used, and are still used. Their advantages? They are portable (try using a computer in the bath), cheap, and have sensory appeal to some writers (yellow legal pads and 2B pencils are a particular favourite). Roald Dahl worked with pencil and paper in his garden shed, a plank of wood for a desk. A novelist friend of mine writes in longhand in bed between midnight and 3 a.m. I am typing this straight on to a computer, using notes from my trusty red exercise books.

The hardware of writing is largely irrelevant: it is the software (or what in modern computer jargon is being called 'wetware' – the human brain) that counts. An expensive desk and computer won't help you write (as the best-selling author Sue Townsend discovered when she still found herself drawn back to the kitchen table). Don't be misled by technology – a writer is someone who writes. Experiment by all means, find a medium that suits you, and then get on with the task of writing your novel.

Key idea

Whether you prefer to write by hand or on a computer, the most important thing to do is just sit down and **write**.

A writer in search of an idea

So, you have cleared a space on the table, bought your paper or polished the screen of your computer. Now what? There are two ways of looking at this. If you want to be a writer, but have nothing to write about, you'll be like a knight in armour searching for a damsel in distress to rescue. Good luck – there is no guarantee you'll find one. There was a six-month gap between finishing my second novel and starting my third novel during which time I had no ideas at all. In desperation, I scraped around in the department of my brain marked 'good ideas', and eventually came up with a scenario anyone who has read *Crime and Punishment* will recognize. And so I filled a notebook with storylines, flogging this dead horse with diminishing enthusiasm, until one day I forgot to pick up the notebook. About time, too.

It's a frustrating fact of the creative life that motivation alone isn't enough to produce a work of art. We need a spark, a germ, a seed. A novel is not a machine – you can't build one. A novel is more like a bonfire: you can lay as much firewood as you please, but without a spark you'll get no heat. Henry James called this spark a *donnée*, a gift, something that you receive.

On the other hand, if you are a person who has an urge to bring into existence an idea which has been bothering you, somebody who has a particular story to tell, thank your lucky stars – you have received your *donnée*, your subject has chosen you.

Focus point

Keep writing something while you're looking for your idea – your diary, personal letters, character studies, plot outlines – nothing is ever wasted, and you never know, the idea might emerge from one of them.

TAKE WHAT YOU GET

Don't resist being chosen. I see it a lot with my students: an idea tugs at their sleeve, but they ignore it because they want to write something more noble, or exciting or intellectual. And generally the results are what you would expect: strained and artificial. But when students recognize the wealth of material they already possess, they can access their greatest asset as writers: their uniqueness. Nobody has lived your story, nobody has had your combination of experiences. Use your life experiences. If you're lucky, you may find you don't have any choice – hopefully your story is demanding to be written.

Bruce Duffy

'You know, you don't always have a choice what you're going to write. You're not like a cow that can give cream with one udder and milk with another.'

HOPING, WAITING AND LOOKING

What can be done if you have an urge to write, but have yet to be chosen by your subject? You can hope, and you can wait, and you can look. There is no shortage of material out there, it's just a matter of adjusting your story antennae to 'ultrasensitive'. We are inundated with story stimulus, perhaps the richest source being life itself: real things happening to real people. Form the habit of watching events through a novelist's eye, listening to dialogue through a novelist's ear.

Trawl through your past for story fodder. Particularly if you are writing for children, think back to the events which were important for you at that time of life. The chances are, if they were important for you, they would be relevant to a young reader.

Newspapers and magazines are often a rich source of material. Rather than storing this material away in your memory, or building a stack of newspapers, or files of unsifted clippings, try keeping a scrapbook. Cut out interesting items from newspapers, or photographs of people and scenery that catch your eye. Much of it may never be used, but what you do use can be invaluable.

When I was writing my first novel I looked out for faces in magazines which fitted my protagonists. The pictures I settled on – the actors Trevor Howard and Meryl Streep – not only helped me in my characterization, but also provided me with the harmless fantasy of casting these actors in the film version of the book!

 Snapshot

If you are looking for an idea, trawl though newspapers. Although the news they usually report is grim, there is little doubt that the stories often have dramatic potential. See what you can make of one of the following, all of which are real examples:

- A six-year-old girl threw herself in front of a train and killed herself because she wanted to become an angel and look after her sick mother.
- A man kidnapped the son of a millionaire friend because he was missing his own children.
- A man and a woman who met as strangers discussed their separate domestic problems and decided to kill themselves.

A less unwieldy tool in the writer's kit is the notebook – no need for scissors and paste here, just a pen and paper. Jot down snatches of dialogue – both heard and imagined. Write down story ideas and fresh twists in the plot. Sketch maps of the imagined landscape, draw pictures of the house your hero lives in. Some novelists always have a notebook handy, just in case an idea comes when they're away from their desk (which, even for the most assiduous writer, is most of the time). Although non-notebook novelists (such as myself) may admire their more efficient brethren, as long as the ideas are written somewhere (and yes, we *do* use the backs of envelopes), they are safe from the vagaries of the writer's mind: a poor memory.

 Key idea

Never go anywhere without a pen and paper. It is at the planning stage that ideas can strike without warning, particularly when you are in the bath, or half asleep, or just about to jump on a bus.

Don't rely on your memory: you may think you can remember it all, but this is the world of dreams we are talking about, and dreams are notoriously difficult to recall. And dreams *are* useful. If you are a vivid dreamer, get in the habit of keeping a dream diary. I often have story dreams in which I am reading children's books. Although most of the ideas don't survive the transition of daylight mentality (being just too way out), those that do have a quirky appeal which is difficult to capture in daylight hours.

I've heard of one writer who uses verbal slips and misreadings to generate ideas. The other day I misheard a passing remark which struck me as having story potential: 'Keep the good worm up,' one man said to another. The mind boggles.

A recent discovery of mine is the spell checker on my computer, which, when it fails to recognize words, will supply substitutes. In this way, my wife's name – Sahera Chohan – was transformed to 'Sacra Choral', which gave me a delightful name for a character I have used in a children's novel.

Focus point

If you have the storyteller spirit, ideas will come along. They may not be quick, and they may not come as expected, but in my experience, they *do* come. Don't lose hope.

GENERATING IDEAS

A more active way of listening out for stories is by doing timed writing exercises. Ideas for stories can be generated by the act of writing itself. One thought can follow another, and before you know it, you have your *donnée*. It is worth realizing that this sort of exercise works best if it isn't goal-oriented. If you're consciously looking for an idea, it may elude you.

Write

This is a very simple and effective technique. Set yourself a time to write – anything from ten minutes to a couple of hours – then, come what may, write about anything that comes to mind. Write about last night's dream. Write about a recent important event. Write about the room you're in. If you're resistant and blocked, write about that.

This exercise is not an end in itself, so write quickly and unselfconsciously. It doesn't matter about the quality of what you produce – nobody will see it. Ask your internal critic to step back so you can exercise that most important of writer's muscles – the brain.

You may be out of condition and find you get quickly exhausted. If this is the case, set yourself an achievable target, and then expand the amount of time you spend writing, perhaps by five or ten minutes every day.

It is also useful to vary the times you write. Set yourself the task of writing for ten minutes first thing in the morning, or last thing at night. Write on the bus on the way to work. Write when you're drunk or sleepy or in a bad mood. If you only write in ideal conditions and when you feel like it, you will be like a painter with a restricted palette. You might paint good stories, but they will always lack something.

Two things to remember:

1 Write for the length of time you said you would – certainly no less. This is a *timed* exercise.

2 Don't read what you've just written. Put it away for a week or two before you read it over. If you don't do this, the exercise may become goal-oriented, and you may fence in your imagination.

Workshop

How will you know if your story idea is any good? There is no way of telling, short of writing it, but try asking yourself these questions:

- How excited am I by it? If it is an idea-led story, do I care enough about the issues it deals with to stay with it for six months, a year, two years?
- If it is a character-led story: do I have at least one vivid, compelling character?

Motivation is the key to seeing through the long process of writing a novel. Often we keep our desires as writers secret – even from ourselves. If your desire is buried, so too will be your motivation. Write a letter to yourself, imagining that an understanding and supportive other part of you will read it. Outline the reasons you want to write, being as honest and as ambitious as you want. Keep the letter in a safe place and read it whenever your motivation flags.

List the reasons why you want to tell this story in particular.

What about subject matter? Some subjects sell well, some are old hat, but an idea alone won't disqualify – or assure success for – a novel. There are no 'off' subjects, no matter how taboo, or how many times they have been written about. Look at the variety of successful novels: though there are trends, they are very general indeed. Originality counts for something, but that doesn't mean the rewriting of an existing story counts for nothing. Don't think of the market at this stage. At the beginning, the person you should be thinking of is yourself. Does the story appeal to you? It is you, after all, who will have to write it. And if a story doesn't excite you, do you really think it will excite someone else?

Snapshot

Choose a favourite novel, and read it again – either in whole, or in part. Why is it your favourite novel? Be as specific as you can. What can you learn from it in terms of the novelist's craft?

 ## Patricia Highsmith

'The first person you should think of pleasing, in writing a book, is yourself.'

Research

When you have your spark, then what? The chances are that a certain amount of research will be needed. 'Write about what you know' is an oft-quoted maxim, but what does it mean? Not that you should restrict yourself to autobiography, never straying outside the bounds of your personal experience. If this were so, we would have no Shakespeare, probably no thrillers, and certainly no science fiction. 'Write about what you know' means *do your research*. Some subjects will need less research than others, and for a beginner this may be a significant advantage, but there are no out-of-bound subjects as long as you know what you're talking about. Don't hurry over this stage in your rush to get ahead – the informed reader may find mistakes, and even the casual reader may find the story lacks credibility and depth.

There are two sorts of research needed: external and internal. External research means collating facts about the fictional world you are about to conjure up. If your setting is unfamiliar to you, you need to know about the landscape and weather and culture of the place. If your story features somebody whose background is not your own, you will need to do some homework so that they are convincing. If you know little about the issues covered by your book, do your reading, and speak to people who do know.

Internal research is the sort you do without leaving your writing desk. Unless you fully imagine your characters, and how they would react in certain situations, your story might lack depth. Internal research means thinking up their biographies, the sort of people they are; getting to know them. This is my favourite form of research, because it means daydreaming, letting your imagination go. Steep yourself in the reality of the story, try to see the world through the eyes of your characters. If anyone thinks you're asleep, shoo them away and tell them you're working.

How to do external research? The Internet is an obvious place to start, but remember that not all the information on the web is accurate. Spread your net wider, so that you get confirmation of what you've found online. Enrol your local librarian into your project, and complete a reading list together. Other novels on the same subject are often a good source of detail, as well as the more obvious reference books. Target people who you think have some of the answers, screw your courage to the sticking point (if you're as nervous as I am), and interview them. Try to visit the location of your story to get the feel of the place.

Bringing your story into focus

There are five questions you can ask to help bring your story into focus: what, how, when, who, why? Let's take these in order.

WHAT SORT OF STORY?

Do you decide on the type of book you want to write before you begin: short story, novella, full-length novel, doorstopper? Comedy, romance, tragedy, farce? Every writer will answer differently – for me, I have a picture of the completed book in my mind before I begin. Somehow questions of form have a habit of answering themselves.

Michael Frayn

'The form chooses you, not the other way round. An idea comes and is already embodied in a form.'

9

HOW DO I START?

I am very visually oriented as a writer, and also a lover of cinema, so I like to imagine the scenes unfolding in front of my eyes. I imagine myself in a comfy chair, in a cinema. The lights go down, the credits roll – what do I see? And then what, and then what? When I reach the end of a scene I ask my cinematic sense to tell me what is required next. I rarely fail to get a picture come to mind.

The problems with this are twofold: first, novel and film are different media with different requirements. Some stories transfer well from one to the other; however, there is no guarantee of this. In fact, the surrealist film director Luis Buñuel used to say that only bad novels could be turned into good movies.

The second problem is in recycling cinematic clichés. Anybody who has taught English to schoolchildren will know that when you set them a story to write, it is not unusual for them to recycle what they saw on television the night before.

So, be aware that it is a novel you are writing, not a screenplay, and that just because a picture comes to mind it doesn't mean it's the right one. However, if you are having difficulty moving the action forwards, try closing your eyes and visualizing each scene. At this stage, don't worry about comprehensibility – you can edit the day's shoot once you have the rushes in.

WHEN DOES THE STORY BEGIN?

Sometimes there will be no doubt in your mind. Sometimes – particularly when the story spans years – it may not be obvious. Should you start at the beginning of your character's life, or begin when the main action takes place? There are two main options for handling time:

1 Establish the background (briefly or at length), and then introduce the first important event which precipitates the action, continuing chronologically.

2 Begin at the event and, while progressing chronologically, feed in the 'backstory' – the necessary history which places the hero or heroine in context. This is the most striking way to begin a story. Franz Kafka's 'Metamorphosis' begins with a bang: 'As Gregor Samsa awoke one morning from uneasy dreams he found himself transformed in his bed into a gigantic insect.'

A third, lesser, option of starting at the end, and then telling the entire story as flashback, is a variation on the two above. Vladimir Nabokov begins *Lolita* this way; the first, short, chapter ends: 'You can always count on a murderer for a fancy prose style. Ladies and gentlemen of the jury, exhibit number one is what the seraphs, the misinformed, simple, noble-winged seraphs, envied. Look at this tangle of thorns.'

Chapter 2 of the novel then begins: 'I was born in 1910, in Paris.'

If you decide to fill in some of the background, the question is how much to give? Although there are no rules for this, if the event which begins the story (the 'trigger', a term which will be explained in Chapter 3) is not in the first two or three chapters, your readers may become restless. The background of a story is like the backdrop in the opera: interesting perhaps, and able to hold the viewer's attention for a while, but if the overture is too long people will start shuffling in their seats. Most people read stories for the action, not the scenery.

Disrupting the chronology of the story, for instance by starting at the end, or using flashback or time slips is a technique that many writers have used, for example Joseph Conrad in *Nostromo*. This is very tricky, however, and should be used only with good reason. Most novels progress chronologically, and most readers are happy with that.

Snapshot

Write the numbers from 1 to 20 on a large sheet of paper, and fill in as many gaps as you can. If you know how the story starts, that is number 1. If you know how it ends, that is 20. You probably won't be able to fill in all 20, but it will give you a sense of structure and balance.

Index cards are useful in structuring the story. Write down as many plot events as you can on individual cards, and then you can change the order if necessary as the story comes into focus. Charlie Chaplin did this – the genius of apparent improvisation and spontaneity was, in fact, a rigorous planner.

Write

Now try writing the first page of your story.

Edit

When you have a story opening you're happy with, rewrite it! Start right at the beginning. Start slap bang in the middle of the action. Start at the end and hint at what has come before. See which version you find the most exciting and intriguing.

WHO BEGINS THE STORY?

The question of who you choose as your hero or heroine will be looked at in Chapter 7. The person who begins the story need not be your protagonist – in fact, there is dramatic advantage in delaying his or her entrance. J. R. R. Tolkien did this to good effect in *The Lord of the Rings*, building up the character of Aragorn so much that, by the time he was introduced, we could almost hear the drum roll.

WHY A NOVEL, WHY *THIS* NOVEL?

The most difficult question, and in some senses the most important, is *why*? Although you may not be able to supply a coherent answer, it is a question worth asking, because tucked within it are other questions of importance, such as: is this the best form for the telling of my tale? Do I have enough material for a novel?

Snapshot

Some novelists manage to write more than one story at a time – rare birds indeed. If you have more than one idea on the go, or are contemplating several ideas, jot down the outline of each. Which idea does your instinct draw you to? What are the reasons not to begin with this one? Which part of yourself do you want to listen to – heart or head?

The point of readiness

When is the point you are ready to start the writing? You've amassed a certain amount of research, developed the plot to a degree, have begun to know your characters. At what point do you roll that crisp white paper into the machine and make the first indelible mark? Everyone will be different. Personally, I like to let the energy of my story build until it reaches critical mass, and something has to give. The first word appears, not when I've completed the research, or have every plot event in place – this could take for ever. I begin a story when it demands to be written, and this is usually when the characters have begun to live. At this point there is a kind of explosion, albeit quiet, and the story makes a quantum leap between domains. Collation becomes creation, the story is being born. It is both frightening and exciting, for up to this point I have just been preparing to be a writer. Now, I *am* a writer.

Key idea

You can start writing whenever it feels right to you to do so. Remember, you don't have to use the early material in the final version, in fact nobody need ever see it, so feel free to plunge into writing.

If you allow the idea to build to this point of critical mass, you can find that it begins to take on a life of its own. The novel, in some sense, already exists and it's just for you to write it.

A. S. Byatt

'It was as if the novel was already written, floating in the air on a network of electrons. I could hear it talking to itself. I sensed that if I would but sit and listen, it would come through, all ready.'

How long is the gap between idea and first word? How much time between germination and the appearance of a seedling? In my experience, it can take anywhere between a couple of months to a year or so. This doesn't mean I am doing nothing other than thinking about the project; often I'm busy with something else. It does mean I'm keeping the idea watered and fed, occasionally checking on its progress. As time passes, so the idea grows and I give it more attention. I don't like to hurry things, but we are all different. There is no formula for this – the thing to remember is that the seed requires a certain respect from the writer. Don't force it, otherwise you may kill it off. And neither water it too little nor too much, otherwise its leaves will wither or its roots will rot. It is a matter of balancing preparation and spontaneity: if you start too soon, it may be premature and you could get lost in the story; too late and you may have no enthusiasm left. Trust your instinct. Remember, a novel isn't a machine, nor is a novelist a mechanic.

Somewhere in here you will realize that any more time spent thinking about the project is procrastination and the only thing left to do is make that first mark on the paper. You may have a fair idea of where you're going, or almost none at all. You will never be perfectly ready, because you can never be fully informed. The only way to find out what happens in the story is to write it.

 ## Thomas Keneally

'Starting a novel is like going to a football match. You may know beforehand what the ingredients are but you still can't tell beforehand what's going to happen. The only way you can resolve the issue is by playing it.'

So you uncap your pen or plug in your computer. You take a deep breath or two, pour your libations or cross your fingers and say to yourself, 'OK, I know I don't know what I'm doing, but I've got to start somewhere', and then you fall forwards into the story. And as long as you keep the words coming, they will find their way on to the page, and if you can do this enough – falling, falling, falling – you'll find you've written something which looks like a novel.

Keep it to yourself

In the early life of a novel, I recommend that you keep the idea to yourself. Not to keep it a secret, but because the creative process is private and fragile: premature exposure can kill it off. If anyone asks what you're working on, be vague. It's not that anyone is going to steal your idea (probably), but that your excitement for a project can dissipate if you spread it around too much. One writer likened talking about a novel in progress to watering the garden with a hose and running a bath at the same time: you may find the water pressure drops. Feedback is essential, but now is not the time for it: anything less than a ringing endorsement could fatally wound your passion. Resist the temptation to talk about it – there is plenty of time to harden it up and show it to the world.

Focus point

Don't look for feedback in the early stages of writing your novel. Keep it quiet until it has grown a bit more resilient.

Office hours and the muse

Hopefully you will be so passionate about your novel, it will cause you to lose sleep, to forget to eat, and dominate your thoughts day and night. I hope when you sit at your desk words fly from the end of your fingers like sparks. If that is the case for you, ignore this section. For the rest of us, if you want to finish your novel in anything under a decade, you will have to write when you don't feel like it. This means discipline and routine.

Most full-time writers report keeping something approximating office hours, even if it means working the night shift. This is partly true for me, and partly not. Certainly, writing is my job, and that involves getting out of bed when I would rather stay in it. However, one of the pleasures of fiction writing is precisely that it is *not* a job. Not that it doesn't require discipline and effort, but that the qualities that stand you in good stead in the office: diligence, trustworthiness, punctuality, efficiency, sociability, co-operation, aren't of much use in the fantastic interior of your novel. There is no point in staring at the page when your brain cells have clocked off and gone home.

Katherine Anne Porter

'Writing is not a business. Writing is an art.'

A novelist is not a clock-watcher. Sometimes you will write for far longer than you expected, sometimes far shorter. The muse cannot be commanded, promoted or sacked. With training she will be less capricious: if you set yourself a target number of words, or a goal of a certain number of hours, and stick to it, you will find her less unruly. But, in the end, she is her own mistress. Sometimes she will dance only if asked nicely and fed coffee and biscuits. Sometimes she will demand attention when you would rather not give it. Try to tame her of course, but likewise respect her whims, for without her, words will turn to sawdust in your mouth. Follow her lead as much as you can. Coleridge regretted all his life that he allowed the man from Porlock to interrupt him in the writing of his famous poem *Kubla Khan*.

 Key idea

Try to set aside some regular time to write, but don't worry if you don't produce Man Booker-winning stuff every time. Some days will be better than others, but as long as you keep at it, you'll get there.

How will I know when I've finished?

Don't think about the end of the book. If your manuscript grows beyond 50,000 words, it will have the necessary bulk to be called a novel. This process may take you three weeks (as Jack Kerouac took with *On the Road*), it may take 12 years (as did Keri Hulme with *The Bone People*). It may finish with a clap of thunder, it may – God forbid – never finish at all. Now is not the time to worry about any of this. A novelist is an underwater swimmer, sometimes coming up for air, but most of the time swimming in the watery depths of the imagination, just making one stroke after another.

Practise, practise, practise

Writing is not just an art – it is also a craft. Our artistic ability may be given, something we are born with. Our ability as craftspeople, we are certainly not born with: *this* we have to learn. Although some of us learn quicker than others, there is only one way to learn a craft: by practice. And the more you practise, the more you will become a master of the form and discover that words do your bidding like willing servants. The more time you spend at your desk, the less time you will gaze out of the window scratching your head. Set yourself a routine and support yourself to keep to it. Even ten minutes a day is worth doing.

There is a common belief that because most of us are literate and fluent, there is no need to serve an apprenticeship if we want to become a successful wordsmith. We all use language, we've read enough novels, surely it's just a matter of starting at the beginning and carrying on until we reach the sign that says: THE END? That's what I thought until I tried to write my first novel. I soon learned that a novel, like a piece of furniture, has its own set of requirements – laws of construction that have to be learned. Just because I had read plenty of novels didn't mean I could write one, any more than I could make a chair because I had sat on enough of them.

Next step

In this chapter we have learned the importance of training ourselves to see the story potential in everything around us. We've also seen that the muse can be a capricious character, and that writing a novel is a feat of endurance, but that with a bit of grit and a regular writing routine, we can build up the stamina necessary to tell the stories only we can tell. In the next chapter we'll be looking at plot, and how to capture and hold your audience's attention.

2

Plot

The three functions of storytelling

What are the functions, for the reader, of storytelling? Although people would express their reasons in a variety of ways, they mostly fall into three groups:

1 entertainment
2 to escape from an onerous or anxious life
3 to understand more of the world.

We all know the excitement to be gained from a well-told story, the pleasure of losing ourselves in a book, or of letting slip our worries for a while. And whether or not we are aware of it happening, stories shape our perception of the world. Life is confusing, sometimes threatening; the story can either help us evade this grim fact or help us get to grips with it.

There is a basic human need for fiction, a need which comes on the heels of our primary requirements of food, clothing, shelter and company. There have been storytellers since people had full enough bellies to stop and think for a moment. And whether the tale is told around a campfire or in the pages of a book, the audience is seeking the fulfilment of these same three needs: entertainment, escape and understanding.

Not all stories will meet these requirements: some are entertaining and nothing else, some leave us more confused than when we started them, some are heavy on understanding and light on everything else. The most enduring stories, those which last over time and are told again and again, fulfil all these requirements: ripping yarns which transport us to another world before bringing us back home with a deepened understanding of this world.

 Ursula Le Guin

'The story – from Rumplestiltskin *to* War and Peace *– is one of the basic tools invented by the human mind, for the purpose of gaining understanding. There have been great societies that did not use the wheel, but there have been no societies that did not tell stories.'*

 Snapshot

Spend some time writing about the things *you* want from a story.

Holding the reader's attention

Unless the reader's attention is held, the three functions described above will never happen. It matters little how profound your understanding, how interesting your ideas, how exciting your climax, if there is no one turning the page.

 Focus point

A novel, we must realize, fully exists only when it is in the hands of a reader. Until that moment, it is only a potential book.

HOW TO GET THE READER TO TURN THE PAGE

This is very simple, and like many simple things, very difficult to do. The reader's attention will be held mostly by the author raising intriguing questions and delaying their answers. If you raise a good enough question at the beginning of a 400-page novel, the reader will wade through almost anything to find the answer. (Beware though: if you make the journey too arduous or boring, he or she will probably turn to the back page to find the answer.) Although a single important question may be enough motivation for a novel, significant questions should be raised in every chapter. However, it is no good raising questions if they are immediately answered: part of the reader's pleasure, of course, is in the delay.

Charles Reade

'Make 'em laugh; make 'em cry; make 'em wait.'

Key idea

Readers turn the page because they care what happens to the characters in the story. They will want a happy outcome for a sympathetic character, but equally they will be hoping that an unsympathetic character gets their comeuppance.

SUSPENSE AND MYSTERY

Narrative questions are of two types: suspense and mystery:

- **Suspense** Questions which look forwards into the future for their answer.
- **Mystery** Questions which look backwards into the past for their answer.

The question that suspense raises is: what happens next? That of mystery is: how did we get into this mess? Mystery is perhaps the more sophisticated of the two, inviting the reader to solve a tricky puzzle. Suspense is more barefaced: this is how life operates – unexpected things happen and we have to take action.

Write

Set aside half an hour or so and write down as many intriguing questions as you can. They could be mystery questions, like 'Who keeps throwing eggs at the vicar?', or suspense questions like 'What would happen if the cats revolted?' For each question, try to come up with at least three possible answers. Then pick the one that appeals to you most and turn it into a short story.

Taken to the extreme, suspense results in the 'thriller' genre – stories which put the hero or heroine repeatedly in danger. The mystery story has developed, at the other end of the scale, into the 'whodunit' – a story which begins with a dead body and works backwards through time until the cause of the death is found. Although these genres focus on their respective questions, both types of question – suspense and mystery – are to be found in almost all fiction. Suspense and mystery can, of course, be used as cheap tricks, but so too can they be used as the foundation for great fiction. Shakespeare, Dickens, Dostoevsky, Joseph Conrad, Thomas Hardy were all masters of the intriguing question.

Key idea

A storyteller who believes that depth of theme or brilliance of style excuses him or her from raising questions and delaying their answer may be in danger of the cardinal literary crime: boring the readers.

David Lodge

'A solved mystery is ultimately reassuring to readers, asserting the triumph of reason over instinct, or order over anarchy.'

What is a plot?

Part of the problem we have with plotting is our lack of clarity about exactly what a plot is. We have read enough books and seen enough films to have an instinct for it, but rarely is instinctual plotting successful.

Focus point

A novel is like a long journey: unless we are very sure of the route and where we are going, we will probably get lost. Part of the fun of such journeys can be in getting lost, but it is more often disheartening – in my third novel I had to throw away six months' work because I took a wrong turning.

The first distinction we need to make is between plot and story. Distinguishing between these two will save many an apprentice writer from wandering too far from the road. We have E. M. Forster to thank for so simply expressing the difference:

Let us define a plot. We have defined a story as a narrative of events arranged in their time-sequence. A plot is also a narrative of events, the emphasis falling on causality. 'The king died and then the queen died' is a story. 'The king died, and then the queen died of grief' is a plot. The time-sequence is preserved, but their sense of causality overshadows it.

Causality is when one event makes another happen. It is these links between events which makes the difference between a collection of anecdotes (that is, a 'story' in Forster's terms) and a novel. Although a story may be interesting, it is rarely as satisfying as a well-constructed plot. Why? Because without causality, there are usually no answers to the questions 'what happens next?' and 'how did we get into this mess?'

Young children have no sense of plot. Listen to their stories: 'This happened and then this happened and then this...' Love them though we may, there is only so much prattle we can listen to before we tire, for there is no causality in their story, nothing to link these events together. More than the events themselves, it is the links we find compelling: who did what to whom and, most importantly, why.

A plot is like a knitted sweater – only as good as the stitches. Without the links we have a tangle of wool, chaotic and uninteresting. Knitting and purling is a start, but it is not everything. Shape is important, too. It is not usually enough to write a series of anecdotes, regardless of their interest, for it is pattern which the eye seeks. Thus 'The king died, and the queen died of grief', apart from raising no immediate questions, still does not qualify as a plot.

So, what is a plot?

A classical plot is a narrative of causality which results in a completed process of significant change, giving the reader emotional satisfaction. It is worth pulling apart this definition to examine its constituents.

First, we are talking about classical plots here. Not that this means the characters have to speak in Greek, but that the structure is based upon a global tradition of storytelling rather than seeking to forge a form of its own. The vast majority of stories are classical in this sense.

A process is an event which occurs in time, and therefore has three aspects: a beginning, a middle and an end. One of the most common reasons for stories failing is the absence of one of these aspects – usually the middle. E. M. Forster's third version of his tale remedies this omission: 'The queen died, no-one knew why, until it was discovered it was through grief at the death of the king.' This has a beginning (the queen dying), a middle (the investigation) and an end (the discovery). And so we have the makings of a murder-mystery with a romantic twist in the tale. Far from brilliant, perhaps, but an improvement on 'The king died and then the queen died.'

This process should be complete. A story has no ending other than that of the teller running out of anecdotes. It is a straight line, proceeding into infinity. A plot, however, is a series of loops, very often coming back on itself to complete its journey:

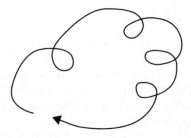

Completion doesn't mean that all the ends should be neatly tied, but that the reader should be able to answer the major questions raised by the author (in this instance: 'Why did the queen die?'). The answers should either be explicit (as it is here: 'Through grief at the death of the king') or implied. If the reader cannot answer the question, once given all the information, he or she will be confused and dissatisfied. There is an unspoken contract between reader and writer: I will raise questions, the author says, and by the end of the book supply the solution. Failing to supply a solution is a recipe for a disgruntled reader.

The completed process should involve change which is significant. Stories are a bit like life: events just happen, one after the other. Sometimes there is pattern, but mostly there isn't. (Although I have a writer friend whose life is like a plot, one coherent adventure after another which she uses for her next novel – how I envy her!) A plot involves change in the life of the hero or heroine, and change which is something other than random. Of course, the change doesn't have to be in the outer world: many stories leave their characters in the same situation in which they were found. But if there is no external change, it must be inside, for change there must be. The central character should be a different person at the end of the tale – if only sadder and wiser. If the novel charts the journey of characters from point A to point B, B can be anything: happy, sad, up, down. Anything, that is, apart from one thing: A. If the characters are left where they began, the reader will say: 'Nice scenery, but so what? We didn't go anywhere.'

Focus point

Although the diagram above shows the plot looping back on itself, this is not the same as arriving back at A, because something, either internal or external, has changed during the journey. If we start with the queen on her deathbed, and return there for the final scene, then we must have learned why her grief was so overwhelming.

The result of this journey should be capable of *emotionally satisfying* us. Classic fiction, even of the highest calibre, should be an emotional experience. Not that it needs to be cathartic (literally 'purging the emotions by tragedy'), nor grandly emotive, but it should appeal first to the heart and then to the head. If the head is the prime target, perhaps an essay would be the better vehicle. And although we may be unsettled by a novel, weep our way through it or be driven to outrage, the overall emotion we feel when we close its cover should be one of satisfaction. If you quiz a reader about the source of this pleasure, they may mention setting, characterization, the author's style; however, if you dig deeper you may find it is simply their enjoyment of answering a question that was raised in the story. This satisfaction is, at heart, what I think almost all readers are looking for. A good answer to a narrative question is as satisfying as scratching an itch.

THERE IS ONLY ONE STORY

All classic stories, whether they qualify as plots or not, are quests. Somebody wants something and goes on a journey to get it. The thing being sought will be different from story to story – some quests are for survival, some for money, some for relationships, some to return to normal. The characters either succeed, or fail, or get something between the two. Full stop.

> ## Key idea
>
>
>
> Not every character embarks on their quest willingly. Some are forced into it by circumstances or set out against their better judgement.

The basic requirements for a plot

A good story needs a plot, and a good plot needs interesting questions and plausible answers, and four basic requirements:

1 AT LEAST TWO CHARACTERS

As human beings are your audience, they are your subject. Even though your characters may be disguised as computers (Hal from *2001: A Space Odyssey*), seagulls (*Jonathan Livingstone Seagull*), rabbits (*Watership Down*) or aliens (*E.T.*), they are in effect human, or quasi-human. Just as there is only one story, so there is only one subject matter of fiction: the human condition. A plot, therefore, needs people.

Why two characters? Why not just one against the world? For two reasons: the first is because personal relationships are at the heart of the human condition, even if only by their absence. There is nothing so necessary for psychic health as other people – even Robinson Crusoe needed Man Friday. A world without other people would be barren and featureless. (I have yet to come across a story with only one character. Stories featuring the last man on Earth, or in the case of Paul Sayer's *The Comforts of Madness*, a catatonic hero, are populated by other people in the form of memories.)

The second reason you need at least two characters is because your job as a writer is to make life difficult for your characters, and there is no greater source of difficulty than other people. Hell, as Jean-Paul Sartre wrote, is other people.

Snapshot

Sit for five minutes and write down the most memorable characters you can recall from films, books, plays or television. Don't stop, just keep writing. Now go back and think about what makes those characters so special?

2 A PROTAGONIST OR PROTAGONISTS

A classic plot needs to have an identifiable protagonist, the focus of attention – the who of the story. There are three options available: single, dual and multiple. More will be said of this in Chapter 7.

3 AN ISSUE WHICH INVOLVES CONFLICT

If a hero attains the goal of his quest immediately, there is no story. Therefore, we need obstacles on the way – people, things, events which block his smooth progress. A plot is a completed process of change, and important change in the fictional world only comes about though conflict. Things may happen by happy coincidence in your story, but if everything goes the character's way the reader will soon be bored. And if the important change happens easily and with no conflict, the reader will feel cheated. Imagine a story with no locked doors, no nasty surprises, no difficult decisions.

Key idea

Conflict doesn't have to be on a grand scale – war, for instance, or death and destruction. The difficult decisions don't have to be life-or-death. Conflict can be internal or quiet, as in the novels of Anita Brookner, but even so, it must be there.

One of the things many readers seek from books is to understand life better, particularly its frightening or painful or confusing aspects. The first stories – myths – were told for this reason, and things haven't changed that much. If we want to understand our lives, we have to understand conflict.

4 SOME SORTS OF RESOLUTION OF THAT CONFLICT

Resolution requires that all important choices have been made, and there are no significant options left for the protagonist. It is no good finishing a thriller with a loaded gun still in the drawer. Every bullet must be fired, every option exhausted.

Tragedy has traditionally ended in death, which neatly removes the options for at least one character, but beware of using it as an easy escape from a tight corner. Death in itself doesn't resolve the plot, except in a very crude way. If the protagonist is left alive and in the midst of remaining conflict, as is often the case in modern literature, there is an important question the author must ask: has the major conflict been completely or substantially resolved? This may not be immediately apparent, particularly if the conflict is internal. You will know the answer to this only if you know what quest your characters are on. It may be a happy ending with the holy grail having been found; it may be a tragedy, the protagonist's hopes dashed; it may fall between the two, sweet-sour or ironic.

Whichever of the three options is chosen, it doesn't necessarily mean the end of trouble, but the return to some sort of plateau for the protagonist, even if it is lower than where he began. Unless the major conflict is resolved, the plot isn't complete, and your readers will think that the last page has been ripped out of the book.

It is fine to begin a novel with an accident or coincidence – many stories begin this way. However, if the end relies on chance, your reader will probably feel cheated. The ancient Greeks had a theatrical device we call deus ex machina, literally 'god in the machine'. It was a convention used by inferior playwrights who were in such a tangle at the end of the play that only an act of God could sort it out. And thus the audience heard the sound of straining ropes and creaking pulleys and an actor playing a god was lowered on to the stage, where he dispensed summary justice, removed all options from the human players and delivered a platitude or two. Modern equivalents are the cavalry arriving, sundry accidents and diseases, or the heroine waking up to discover it was a dream. I can still remember the shocked disappointment of reading Lewis Carroll's *Alice's Adventures in Wonderland* for the first time:

> 'Wake up, Alice dear!' said her sister.
> 'Why, what a long sleep you've had!'
>
> 'Oh, I've had such a curious dream!'
> said Alice.

Oh no! How could you do this to us, I wanted to cry. You can't paint your character into a corner and then deny the existence of walls and floors.

Two conventions of resolution

There are two conventions of resolution you should know, even if to dismiss them. The first is that of placing the resolution in the hands of the protagonist. There is usually more emotional satisfaction in the protagonist using his or her own skills and resources to resolve the quest than in the all-conquering hero or heroine coming to the rescue. This is particularly important in children's stories, or young-adult fiction where the autonomy of the protagonist is all-important – children want literature which gives them a break from their normal disempowered state. The title of Roald Dahl's book says it all: *Danny the Champion of the World*.

The second convention is what in Hollywood films is called the 'obligatory scene'. This is the meeting of protagonist and antagonist, goody and baddy, in the last reel – the showdown at the OK Corral. Audiences love this, even demand it, as the famously rewritten ending of *Fatal Attraction* demonstrated: the original ending where the psychopathic character played by Glenn Close killed herself was scotched, in favour of Michael Douglas's character doing the deed.

Snapshot

Look back at the list of memorable characters you made earlier in the chapter and note down whether they are protagonists, antagonists or something else. Do you favour the goodies or the baddies?

Sources of antagonism

Just as you need a protagonist, so in order to generate conflict, you need an antagonist. Unless something or somebody opposes the hero's or heroine's will, you will have a story quest which ends before it begins, because there will be nothing between desire and fulfilment. The source of antagonism can exist on three levels.

1 INNER

The inner protagonist lives within the mind of the hero or heroine and takes the form of an uncomfortable emotion. Psychological turmoil usually looks like guilt, shyness, doubt, self-hatred, fear, anger, a broken heart.

Because the novel (and short story) have the facility of eavesdropping on character's thoughts, it is the narrative form most often used in exploring this internal turmoil.

2 INTERPERSONAL

This is conflict between people, arising from the clash of motivations: character A wants one thing, character B wants another thing which is incompatible. Because conflict between people is usually expressed in dialogue form, this second level of antagonism is most often the focus of stage plays.

3 EXTERNAL

External conflict can either be physical, where a character's physical well-being is threatened (burning buildings, poverty, illness) or social, where a character's social status is under duress (disapproval of society, the consequences of breaking the law). Film comes into its own with third-level conflict – *The Towering Inferno* would have been less dramatic as a novel, and positively dangerous as a stage play!

Snapshot

Think about the three types of conflict listed above. Try to think of at least three books, plays or films that fit into each category.

Complexity and complication

Robert McKee has pointed out that shallowness in a story is often the result of pitching conflict solely on one level: the confessional novel in which nothing ever happens, or the stage play in which people do nothing other than row, or the film whose dramatic focus is one car chase after another. Perhaps the most enduring novels are those which pitch conflict on all three levels: *Madame Bovary*, *Wuthering Heights*, *Doctor Zhivago*, *Catch 22*.

It is not the quantity of action which counts, but the quality. A thin plot is not necessarily made more substantial by adding more action. If you sense this is the case in a story you are writing, pause to consider what levels of antagonism you are employing. If most of your conflict is between people, introducing another character whose motivation is different from your central character's will just complicate matters. Try some lateral thinking: how about an act of violence (third-level antagonism), or a sudden loss of nerve of your protagonist (first-level antagonism)? This might add depth to your plot, making it complex rather than complicated.

Write

Although life rarely has a coherent plot, it often has the makings of one. Many novelists use a true event as a starting point for their writing. If you are not already at work on a novel, try this suggestion.

Take an episode in your life which has dramatic potential. Make any changes to it which could improve the structure – perhaps combining two people into one fictional character, or inventing a resolution. Write it out as though it is a synopsis for a plot, then ask yourself these questions:

- Who is the protagonist/who are the protagonists?
- What is the quest?
- Is it more of a mystery or a suspense?
- If you were to write this as a novel, what questions would the events raise? How could you delay their answer?
- What are the sources of antagonism, and on what levels?
- Is it completed, that is, are the major questions answered or answerable given the information?
- What coherent change occurred?

Edit

When you have answered all the questions above, take your synopsis and use it as the basis for a short story.

Next step

In this chapter we have learned how to hold the reader's attention by delaying answers to questions of mystery or suspense. We've touched on the importance of causality and conflict in delivering reader satisfaction. In the next chapter we will take this even further, focusing on the eight-point plot arc and how you can use it to strengthen any story.

3

The eight-point arc

Every classic plot needs to pass through eight phases, what I call the eight-point arc:

1 Stasis

2 Trigger

3 The quest

4 Surprise

5 Critical choice

6 Climax

7 Reversal

8 Resolution.

In this chapter we'll look at each of these in turn and then explore them through a classic tale, *Jack and the Beanstalk*.

The classic plot

1 STASIS

The stasis is the base reality of the tale, the 'once upon a time'. Although the base reality may contain conflict, and indeed an ongoing quest, it is a day much like any other day. Where to start the novel is sometimes a thorny problem. Some novels have an extended stasis (William Styron's novel, *Sophie's Choice*, for instance), while others have only an implied stasis, leaping from the first word into the next stage which is the trigger.

2 TRIGGER

The trigger is an event beyond the control of the hero or heroine which turns the day from average to exceptional. The event may be huge or tiny, it may be pleasant or unpleasant, it may not be recognized as significant at the time; however, from this point onwards, the characters really come alive. Before this time, the characters are in suspended animation, their figurative electrocardiographs registering an unwavering line. The trigger is the first blip on an otherwise stable line.

Focus point

If you choose to start your novel at the trigger point in the story, you can always give the reader information about the stasis situation as part of the backstory. This way your readers will gradually achieve insight into why the protagonist behaves as they do.

3 THE QUEST

The effect of the trigger is to generate a quest for the protagonist. In the case of an unpleasant trigger, the quest is often to return to the original stasis; in that of a pleasant trigger the quest is often to maintain or increase the pleasure. The quest may change throughout the novel. If it does, however, the subsequent quest should incorporate the former, raising the stakes all the time.

Focus point

A story could begin with the quest for money, evolve into a quest for love and, from there, into a quest for survival.

4 SURPRISE

A strong quest is a good start for a story, but as outlined earlier, the characters need to encounter obstacles along the way. At the very least, unexpected things must happen.

Sometimes the surprises will be pleasant, helping the central character on his or her way; more important, however, are the unpleasant surprises. The narrative surprises which move the story forwards are, ironically, those which block the smooth advance of the hero's or heroine's quest. Surprise is conflict made concrete, and may be caused by another person or something in the environment; it may also happen suddenly or as the result of an accumulation of events.

For a narrative surprise to work well requires that we balance two things: unexpectedness and plausibility. A poorly constructed surprise is often predictable, visible from ten pages ahead and boring to wait for. Some easily anticipated 'surprises' are valid – I love slapstick, for instance, but even when you see the custard pie coming, the convention demands that the next one will confound your expectations.

It is no good being unexpected, however, if the surprise wouldn't happen within the bounds of credibility set by the author. Implausibility is when the reader's 'willing suspension of disbelief' (as Coleridge called the reader requirement) is stretched beyond the point of comfort. If a surprise is predictable or implausible, the average reader will feel cheated: this is low-grade storytelling.

Balancing the two things can result in the delightful moment in a story when the reader slaps his forehead and says, 'Of course, I should have realized!'

Key idea

We all know that stories are not literally true, but we put that knowledge to one side so that we can enjoy a fairy story, science fiction or a soap opera. This is what is meant by 'suspension of disbelief'.

5 CRITICAL CHOICE

If the unexpected brick wall in a hero's path is insuperable, he comes to a stop and the story is over. If he is to continue on his quest, however, he needs to change course. In order to surmount the obstacle he has to make a difficult decision – what we can call a *critical choice*. 'What am I going to do now?' he asks. 'How am I going to deal with this problem?'

The word 'drama' is Greek, and means 'a thing done'. Not a thing happening by chance, or a thing being done to another, but the action of human beings when faced with obstacles. What sort of actions do our fictional heroes have to make? They have to make choices, that is, they must respond rather than react. What is the difference? It is a question of decisiveness – the hero or heroine decides, whether consciously or not, to take a certain path, even if the choice is to do nothing. The novelist assumes the existence of free will: our characters may be compulsive, driven, inadequate, and deluded, but they must be seen as responsible for their actions, even if their actions are not enough to achieve what they want. Unless the character is accountable in some sense for his or her actions, we have accident and coincidence and chaos.

Snapshot

Think back over the decisions you have made in your life. What would have happened had you chosen the other path? This could be a big decision, like choosing between two lovers, or it could be something seemingly small, like having cereal rather than toast for breakfast. Try to imagine how those cornflakes could have changed your life.

6 CLIMAX

These critical choices which are forced on the characters come to a head in the form of a *climax*, that is, the decision made manifest. A *surprise* could be a burglar breaking into somebody's house; the *critical choice* of the householder is self-defence the *climax* is the burglar being hit over the head. Sometimes the critical choice and the climax are back to back, seemingly being one action; at other times there could be a long delay.

A narrative surprise is only important according to the difficult decisions that are forced on the character – the reason why pleasant surprises have little place in the forward momentum of the plot. The subject matter of the novel is the human condition, remember: events are interesting only if they profoundly involve the human protagonists. Intrigue and suspense come from the skilful placing of obstacles in the path of your characters and saying 'Get out of that one!'

The point of obstacles is to put your protagonist in a tight corner so that his or her mettle is tested, so that at the end the protagonist emerges a changed person. Therefore, the protagonist should be forced into making a critical choice (that is, a choice made in the midst of crisis) to continue the quest, a choice which will cause a change of direction.

The surprise, critical choice and climax may be spread over a hundred pages, or appear within the same paragraph. Whichever of these, hopefully the reader is deeply involved in the conflict. Although the focus of the novel may be on the surprise or the critical choice, the climax is a necessary part of delivering the goods. A narrative climax, like a trigger or a surprise, is an event – something occurring in the tangible world of things and bodies. Your climax need not be spectacular, but it needs to be visible. The ancient Greek proscription against portraying physical suffering and death on the stage no longer holds. If your novel is the type to include such things, you should include the crashing cars, the blood, the finger pulling the trigger, not for the sake of sensationalism, but because most modern readers demand it. Omitting a climax, or having it reported, as Sophocles and Aeschylus did, you will be in danger of reneging on an assumed promise: that you will not only supply an answer to the question the story raises, but you will show it to us.

The climax is still not the fulfilment of the narrative journey, however. There are still two more steps to climb: the first is what Aristotle called *reversal*.

Focus point

'Show don't tell' has become one of the basic rules of modern storytelling. Whatever happens in your novel, you need to take the reader right into the action.

Write

Pick one of the following dramatic events and write a short passage *showing* (not telling) what happens.

- Every third person on Earth disappears at the same moment.
- All the animals escape from a zoo.
- A huge sinkhole opens up in your town centre.

7 REVERSAL

Aristotle

Aristotle defined a reversal as 'a change from one state of affairs to its opposite ... which should develop out of the very structure of the plot, so that they are the inevitable or probable consequence of what has gone before'. A reversal, in other words, is the consequence of previous events – that is, surprises, critical choices and climaxes.

If the climax does not result in a reversal, a question is raised: is there a purpose to the climax other than as spectacle? 'Spectacle' is action for the sake of action, effect for the sake of effect. Elephants in *Aida*, expensive cinematic special effects, the gratuitous sex or violence scene: these are all examples of spectacle, a dramatic resource which Aristotle understandably placed at the bottom of the list. If the answer to the question about purpose is 'No, I just chucked it in there because it looks good', don't be surprised if some readers feel short-changed. Respect your reader's intelligence enough to realize that few of them will be satisfied with spectacle alone. I'm not necessarily talking about literary fiction here: there is nothing high brow about delivering the reader something which coheres into a plot, rather than the 'And then, and then...' type of story.

If you want to incorporate your narrative climax into the structure, you need to create a reversal from it. Some reversals are immediately apparent (the classic tragic reversal is from being alive to being dead, the biggest status change there is), some are not so.

Your story reversals should be *inevitable* and *probable*. Nothing should happen for no reason; changes in status should not fall out of the sky. The story should unfold as life unfolds: relentlessly, implacably and plausibly.

Focus point

To test whether a climax has been incorporated into the plot, try cutting it out. If it can be removed without any damage to the plot (which is what may happen when an editor sees it), then you haven't managed to construct a reversal that changes the status of the characters.

Inevitability doesn't mean predictability, however. A novel is not a slice of life: it is both more ordered and more unpredictable than that. Predictability has no place in a story: it is what happens before 'once upon a time'. What happens afterwards is drama.

8 RESOLUTION

Resolution has already been spoken of in Chapter 2. It may be apparent now that what we call the 'resolution' is, in fact, a fresh stasis. Our characters return, as it were, to their state of suspended animation, their electrocardiograms finding a new status quo.

Workshop

Analyse a story in progress. Ask yourself these questions:
- What is the trigger?
- What is the protagonist's motivation?
- How does this translate into a quest?
- Is there an escalation of surprises, critical choices and climaxes from minor to grand?

Write

Starting a story is often just a matter of asking 'What if?' If you are not yet working on a novel, try this exercise to get you going. Select one element from each of the following categories (if you want more of a challenge, pick them at random):

Character	bricklayer, lawyer, computer hacker, rich layabout, trapeze artist
Object	razorblade, pocket watch, photograph, bottle of pills, wallet
Setting	remote cottage, library, block of flats, high-tech industrial complex, abandoned warehouse

Put the character (your protagonist) in the situation with the object. Somebody else (the antagonist) is due on the scene. This is the stasis. See if you can imagine a trigger which can generate a compelling quest for the protagonist. What can go wrong? How could it be resolved? If the idea has sufficient life, explore it further to see if you have the makings of a novel.

Grand, major and minor arcs

The eight-point arc is the classic dramatic unit. A narrative can be divided into constituents, from grand (the story as a whole), through major (the dramatic unit called an 'act' in theatre, usually dividing the story into three, four or five parts), to minor (scenes). Each of these units, to conform to the classic model, needs to proceed, in order, through each of the eight stages. Progression may be swift or slow, regular or erratic – this doesn't matter; however, if you sense your novel is going astray, it will often be because one of the stages has been overlooked. Some omissions are obvious, as in the case of a missing resolution. Some are not so obvious – a story, for instance, in which there is no clear reversal. The most commonly overlooked is that of the critical choice.

Grand, major and minor: these are the three levels the eight-point arc relates to. Thus the arc of a plot could be represented like this:

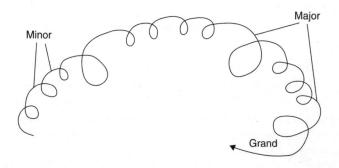

The law of diminishing returns requires that the significance of critical choices, climaxes and reversal increases as the story progresses. If the final critical choice is less challenging than one before it, we may feel let down. If this happens with a climax, the result is plain – anti-climax. Pacing is important, combining allegro with andante, as it were, action with passivity. However, anti-climax is rarely successful. The last part of E. M. Forster's *A Passage to India*, in which the grand climax (the trial of Aziz) is followed by a quiet (though undoubtedly important) third act, is in danger of anti-climax.

Analysis of a story: *Jack and the Beanstalk*

In order to illustrate these ideas, let's strip a well-known fairy story down to its basics and see how it works. Fairy tales are often good models for well-constructed plots: their age and constant retelling have the effect of knocking off any superfluous bits. I have taken the liberty of dividing the story into acts.

APPLYING THE EIGHT-POINT ARC

Children have a very limited attention span, and the stasis of a fairy tale is often a sentence or two: 'Once upon a time there was...' Children are demanding, if sometimes indiscriminate, readers: they don't want background information, they want action. Thus, the plot proper begins with the trigger, 'Milky White gave no milk.' This day is not an average day.

Jack and the Beanstalk

Act I

Once upon a time there was a boy called Jack who lived with his mother. They were very poor. All they owned was a little cottage and a cow called Milky White.

One day Milky White gave no milk. 'There is only one thing to do,' cried Jack's mother. 'You must take the cow to market to sell.'

Off Jack went. On the way he met a strange old man who offered five magic beans for the cow. Jack wasn't sure this was such a good thing, but they were magic beans, so he decided to make the swap.

At home his mother was livid. She threw the beans out of the window, boxed Jack's ears and sent him to bed. Jack was distraught.

Act II

In the morning they saw that a huge beanstalk had grown in the night. Without a second thought Jack climbed the beanstalk and found himself in a land high above his own. He walked to an enormous house and met an ogre's wife. She fed the boy and then

---

hid him when the ogre came in for his breakfast. The ogre could smell the boy, but his wife convinced him that it was last night's supper. After breakfast the ogre fell asleep over his favourite pastime, counting his gold coins. Jack stole the bag of coins and escaped without being detected.

Act III

Eventually the gold coins ran out, so Jack climbed back up the beanstalk. The ogre's wife was less welcoming now – the last time she let a boy in, he stole their money. Jack convinced her that he was not the same boy, and she let him in. Again the ogre smelled Jack, and this time nearly found him. After breakfast, the ogre took out his magic hen, who lays golden eggs on command.

Jack waited until the ogre was asleep and then stole the magic hen. The ogre woke, but Jack escaped easily.

Act IV

Jack decided one day to go on another adventure up the beanstalk. Certain this time that the ogre's wife wouldn't let him in, Jack sneaked into the kitchen. This time when the ogre smelled him, the wife joined in the search, but they couldn't find Jack. After breakfast the ogre took out his magic harp which sang beautiful songs when commanded.

Jack waited until the ogre was asleep and then stole the magic harp. The ogre woke up and chased Jack. He nearly caught him, but Jack was too quick, and reached the bottom of the beanstalk before his pursuer. Jack chopped the beanstalk down, and the ogre crashed to his death.

And, of course, they all lived happily ever after.

The trigger is like a starting pistol signalling the beginning of a hurdle race, in other words the quest – which in this case is to sell the cow. There is no change to the quest throughout all four acts: Jack wants one thing only – money (or, at least, valuable possessions).

In order to give impetus to the quest, solid motivation has to be established. If the protagonist (Jack) doesn't have enough reason to endure this obstacle course, he will give up when the hurdles get uncomfortably high. Thus, in this story, it is important that

Jack and his mother are poor. (They are well off at the end of Act II; that is, until the gold coins run out.) In this regard, this story goes wrong at the beginning of Act IV: there is no reason for Jack to venture into the dangerous arena of the ogre's kitchen – he has a perpetual source of wealth in the hen. His new motivation – greed or inquisitiveness or a yearning for adventure – is less compelling than his original motivation of poverty, and so as adults we may feel less sympathy to his plight. This story could be improved by making it a three-act tale, less repetitive and more symmetrical.

Back in the story, however, some surprises are in store for Jack.

NARRATIVE SURPRISES IN *JACK AND THE BEANSTALK*

The first surprise for Jack is meeting the old man and being offered five magic beans for a cow. If he had met a man who bought the cow for £20, as Jack's mother was expecting, there would have been no conflict and, therefore, no story.

A surprise has two aspects: the set-up and the pay-off. The set-up is the necessary preparation, the laying of clues in the text, so that in retrospect they are seen as causes which may have been overlooked. The set-up for Jack's first surprise, as in all fairy tales, is simple: he has no money and has to sell the cow. The pay-off is the moment of impact, when expectations are confounded. Jack expected to be offered money, and he was offered beans – not just any beans but *magic* beans. In jokes, the pay-off is called the punch line.

The most important surprises in the rest of this tale are divided into two scenes per act: the ogre in the kitchen and the results of Jack stealing from him. These can be broken down as follows:

Act II: the ogre comes into the kitchen and smells Jack.
Act III: the ogre searches for Jack and chases him.
Act IV: the ogre increases his search for Jack and almost catches him.

The protagonist should pass greater and greater points of no return, facing greater dangers and having greater pressure put on his resources. The Jack story does well in this regard. If well constructed, the pay-off can be deeply satisfying to the reader. The delight for children here is the escalating danger of Jack: the pay-off – being hunted and chased – is not far removed from many adult thrillers. However, for most adult readers, a good surprise requires more than shock alone; it needs to do two more things.

1 Give insight into characters

Surprise on its own will have limited effect, except for young children. Only if the pay-off has significance will the adult reader find sustenance in it. One level of significance is that of the characters: if we view people differently as a result of an unforeseen action, we have something to chew on. How will they react? What will they do? The answer to these questions should leave the reader having a deeper understanding of the characters in the tale.

Snapshot

Write a short passage from the ogre's perspective, giving insight into his feelings about Jack and his missing hen.

2 Change the course of the plot

Another, and greater, level of significance is that of the plot. Some surprises in a novel are minor, and have only limited effect; some are the axis of the tale, changing everything that follows. The change should be irresistible and have a certain inevitability about it, as Aristotle said.

Raising questions and then supplying plausible, yet unexpected, answers: this is the job of the storyteller. And a single ingenious surprise is enough to sustain an entire novel. A few writers, mostly enormously wealthy as a result, have built their careers on the success of their surprises: of them Agatha Christie is perhaps their queen. If you want to hear the sound of cash registers ringing, tickle your readers' sense of intrigue and then scratch them in just the right places.

CRITICAL CHOICES IN *JACK AND THE BEANSTALK*

Jack's critical choice in Act I is to sell the cow; his subsequent critical choices are to steal the bag of gold, the hen which lays golden eggs, and finally the magic harp. Fortunately for Jack it seems that he was a greedy little boy with little imagination – no genuine problem deciding what to do. Some more challenging critical choices in well-known stories have been: Romeo stabbing himself on seeing Juliet dead; Juliet taking poison on seeing Romeo dead; Lady Chatterley sleeping with the gamekeeper Mellors; Raskolnikov killing the landlady in *Crime and Punishment*. The more challenging the decision, the greater the dramatic potential.

Snapshot

What would have happened if Jack had decided not to steal the gold, the hen and the harp? Would the ogre have eaten him? Or would they have gone on to become friends?

CLIMAXES IN *JACK AND THE BEANSTALK*

The climaxes of the fairy tale are:

- **1 minor:** to ask for breakfast
- **3 major:** to lie to the wife
             to sneak into the kitchen
             to sell the cow
- **3 grand:** to steal the bag of gold
             to steal the hen
             to steal the harp and chop the beanstalk down, killing the ogre.

REVERSALS IN *JACK AND THE BEANSTALK*

Jack was rich at the end of Act II (the change was from poor to rich, likewise in Act III), not without reason, but because he saw a bag of gold, decided to steal it, and did so. 'Drama' remember, means 'a thing done' – if the ogre had given Jack the money, there would have been no critical choice and therefore no drama. A reversal shouldn't just happen as an act of God.

Robert McKee

'Nothing progresses in a story, except through conflict.'

What is the major reversal of Jack at the end of Act I? He starts the story as the trusty son and ends as the punished son – the 'change from one state of affairs to its opposite' is from approved to disapproved. Remember that the plot is a completed process of change, most importantly the change in character. If your character has no significant reversal, he or she will probably not be more than two-dimensional.

What is the grand reversal of the story as a whole? From poor to infinitely rich, with implications of power – a popular transformation if ever there was one.

Write

Write your own version of *Jack and the Beanstalk*, using the eight point plot arc as described above, but this time write it from the viewpoint of the ogre's wife.

How to use this information

Sometimes this approach to storytelling leaves students cold, and so it should. There is a temptation with such a structuralist approach to think that a novelist is a sort of intellectual engineer: assemble enough parts, follow a blueprint, and there you have it: a mechanism capable of flight – a literature machine. But a novel is not a machine; it is an infinitely complex relationship between author and page, page and reader. Though tempting for a neat mind to design the plot according to the eight-point arc, the control to which we aspire is no more than an illusion. For a novel, unlike a machine, is greater than the sum of its parts.

The components of a successful work of art combine to produce something else, something beyond our control. A novel must somehow generate enough electricity between each of its components so that its engine starts to hum, its propellers turn and it taxies down the runway. How this happens is a mystery to me. How we can get normally sensible and sane people, adults as well as children, to take seriously something which is patently a lie, is beyond my comprehension. And when readers do take a working novel seriously, they feel emotions, sometimes strong emotions, just as they would in real life. I will never cease to be amazed when a reader talks about a scene in a book of mine as though it really happened.

So, how to use this information? Rather than using it to build a story, I find it most useful as a checklist against which to measure a work in progress. If I sense a story is going wrong, I see if I've unwittingly missed out a stage of the eight-point arc. It may not guarantee you write a brilliant story, but it will help you avoid some of the pitfalls of a brilliant idea gone wrong.

 ## Snapshot

Analyse a favourite story according to the eight-point arc.

Next step

In this chapter we have seen how a plot is created from a series of arcs, with the biggest at the end. We've studied the eight phases of the classical plot arc in some detail and by now you should be able to apply this to your own writing. In the next chapter, we are going to see how your plot can be deepened and enriched with the use of subplot and symbolism.

4

Subplot and symbolism

In this chapter we'll be looking at subplot and symbolism. At first sight, this might seem like an odd pairing, but, as we shall see, careful use of each can considerably enrich the reader's experience of a novel, adding to its texture and resonance as well as buttressing its themes.

Subplot

The subplot is a subsidiary storyline which runs parallel to the main story, a narrative strand that can be taken away without causing the whole book to unravel. A novel can have several subplots, developed to greater and lesser extents – and it does have a job to do, other than filling up pages. Although a developed subplot is unlikely in a short story, it is important in a full-length novel, adding substance to the tale and pacing its telling.

SUBSTANCE

The first job of the subplot is to add a dimension to the story which the main plot lacks. Because fiction is a tidied-up version of life, it is easy to stray into a simplistic portrayal of events which does justice neither to the complexity of real life nor to the intelligence of your readers.

 Focus point

One way of visualizing this is by imagining your main character on stage, performing actions under the glare of a single spotlight: the audience will see things clearly enough, but everything will appear flat, all subtle shading and perspectives ironed out.

Subplot often involves minor characters who, as it were, circle the main characters with spotlights showing sides of them of which we were unaware. This can have the effect of throwing features into sharp relief, making the characters three-dimensional – in a word, giving them substance.

The subplot performs this function in one of two ways: resonance or contradiction.

When the subplot resonates with the main plot, it confirms our evaluation of the characters and the meaning we put on their actions – in effect, it says the same thing in a different way. For instance, in *Wuthering Heights*, the subplot of Heathcliff's relationship with the resentful brother Hindley echoes everything we know about him: Heathcliff is wild, impulsive and revengeful. The

Cathy subplot, about her acceptance into polite society and marriage to the doting Edgar, likewise resonates with the main story: they both say the same thing – love is stronger than propriety, passion greater than security. Without the subplot, the main story could have survived, but only just – it would have been thin gruel indeed.

Occasionally, instead of highlighting aspects of the main cast, the subplot throws light on aspects of the theme. In such cases, the theme of the subplot works as an analogy of the main theme, for instance, the Gloucester story in *King Lear*. Here, both men believe the lies told by scheming offspring to the detriment of their unjustly accused loyal child. The theme of the main plot, that of believing flattery at one's peril, is echoed by the subplot.

When the subplot contradicts the main plot its intended effect is often comic. For instance, in Kingsley Amis's *Lucky Jim*, the subplots are strewn with disasters, while the main plot charts the rise and rise of the hero. The hero succeeds, not because of skill or diplomacy – the subplot disabuses us of any thoughts of that – but because he is a lucky Jim.

Focus point

If you are unsure how to construct a subplot, think about the second most important character in your story – often the protagonist's best friend, or arch enemy – and develop a storyline for them.

Write

If you are working on a novel, examine the main plot. Ask yourself what attributes of your main cast need to be highlighted by subplot. Are you going to do this by resonance or by contradiction? Brainstorm a list of ideas for each type of subplot. Take the ones that appeal to you most and write a short scene.

PACE

Subplot also has the less complex function of slowing the progress of the main plot. The subplot can act as a form of prologue, carrying the reader's interest until the trigger occurs – as in William Styron's *Sophie's Choice*, which in effect has a 100-page stasis about the narrator's past and his struggle to be a writer, before the trigger of meeting Sophie occurs. In the case of an extended stasis, the trigger could be back-to-back with the Act I climax.

Subplot is more often found woven within the body of the plot, in which case it can have the function of placing obstacles in the path of the protagonist so that the story doesn't climax too quickly. In *Jack and the Beanstalk*, the subplot of the ogre's wife gives additional interest, teasing the reader with questions: will she let Jack in, will she tell her husband where the boy is hiding? Sometimes there is delicious stress in being made to wait.

MULTIPLE PLOTS AND TWO-HEADED MONSTERS

If a subplot is developed beyond a certain point, it takes on a life of its own, and it will have its own eight-point arc, including a need for a resolution. Beware of developing the subplot too much: you may create a two-headed monster, that is, a story with two distinct plots of equal weight, which can be confusing to the reader. If this happens, you have three options: the first is to reduce the significance of one and increase the significance of the other, establishing an unequivocal top-dog and under-dog story status. The second is to split the book in two and make two novels from it. The third, and most challenging, option is to depart from the classic story structure and form a multiple-plotted novel. Julian Barnes's novel *A History of the World in 10½ Chapters* is an example of this. If such a novel is to be something more than a collection of anecdotes or stories randomly glued together, however, it must relate *thematically*.

Write

Take these one-line synopses (with possible themes in brackets) and invent a subplot to complement them (either by resonance or by contradiction):

- A father and son successfully cope with the aftermath of a divorce, but then the mother fights for custody (love has responsibilities).

- An out-of-work actor impersonates a woman to get work, and becomes a soap-opera star (men are very different from women).

- A young man follows his heart rather than adult expectations (freedom is more important than responsibility).

If you want to see what one story medium has made of these ideas, study the Dustin Hoffman films: *Kramer* vs *Kramer*, *Tootsie* and *The Graduate*, from which I took the outlines. Because of the rigorous financial and technical constraints of cinema, films often display very precise story structures, and as novelists we can often benefit from studying them.

Symbolism

A symbol is anything that stands for anything else. Of course, all language is symbolic – the word 'dog' has never yet bitten anybody – however, the literary forms referred to as symbolism are: metaphor, simile and allegory. Why do we use symbols? There are three reasons:

1 To demonstrate a concept

Drama is the enactment of ideas as narrative, not the presentation of ideas themselves, which, after all, is the domain of non-fiction writing. Symbolic acts clothe abstract or difficult ideas in form, demonstrating a concept without explaining it. A novel which successfully uses symbolic resonance in this way is Ken Kesey's *One Flew over the Cuckoo's Nest*: MacMurphy, the troublesome inmate of the mental asylum, is punished first by electroconvulsive therapy, and then by lobotomy. These acts, though plausible within the story context, and operating on the everyday level of narrative reality, also have echoes of other things: the first of torture, the second of emasculation. Sometimes a symbol can be extended over the course of a novel, in which case it edges towards allegory. For instance, in the Ken Kesey novel, the oppressive State is symbolized by the mental institution which the narrator calls 'the Combine'. Similarly, Joseph Conrad's famously extended symbol, *Heart of Darkness*, draws parallels between Africa and the dark heart of humankind.

2 To add a further dimension

The second value of symbolism is its ability to add a further dimension to dramatic action by drawing parallels between the particular and the universal. Having a strong symbolic element tells us it is more than one person's story. Seeing beyond the surface reality to what lies underneath, as we do with the Ken Kesey book, we realize it is a tale with social relevance, and therefore something which concerns us all. By showing us the link between the microcosm and the macrocosm, the book steps out of the confines of the page and into our lives.

3 To sneak behind the rational mind

The third value of symbolism is harder to grasp. The more we use words, the more we realize their shortcomings. We may be great experts of language, we may have huge vocabularies, however, life, it seems, is forever evading our attempts to capture it with words. Why? Precisely because words are not real – they are signs, conventions, symbols. The job of the writer is to grope towards the truth of a situation, in the full knowledge that he or she will never successfully pin it down in words. Symbols, because they recognize this fact (love is not at all like a rose, nor the moon like a balloon), can approach things side on, sneaking behind the rational mind in the hope of catching us unawares.

> ## ❝❞ Ursula Le Guin
>
> *'I am an artist ... and therefore a liar. Distrust everything I say. I am telling the truth. The only truth I can understand or express is, logically defined, a lie. Psychologically defined, a symbol. Aesthetically defined, a metaphor.'*

But beware: a novelist should make his spade a spade before he makes it a symbol. If it is too obvious or cumbersome, it will undermine the story's credibility, turning it into full-blown allegory, a form with which most modern readers would be uncomfortable. Symbolism works best on a subliminal level. If we notice it, it will have the effect of taking us out of the story, drawing our eye back to the artifice of fiction.

Focus point

Beware of unintentional symbolism. All of the choices you make for your novel have the potential to be symbolic, which is fine as long as you understand what you're doing.

Ray Bradbury

'There are other things of greater value in any novel or story ... humanity, character analysis, truth on other levels... Good symbolism should be as natural as breathing ... and as unobtrusive.'

Key idea

Symbols are used to demonstrate a concept, add a dimension and sidestep the rational.

NAMES

Be aware of the reverberation of meaning, particularly in names and jobs. No names are neutral in fiction – they all carry the weight of their predecessors. A heroine called 'Juliet', or 'Norma Jean' or 'Madonna' will be obviously referential; one called 'Mary' or 'Janet' or 'Anne' less so. Consider names very carefully, and think what resonance they might have (Mary – the Virgin Mary?). Does the resonance suit your intention? Names can be used in several ways:

- **clearly allegorical:** 'Willie Loman' in *Death of a Salesman*, 'John Self' in *Money* by Martin Amis
- **suggestive:** Mr Gradgrind from Dickens's *Hard Times*, Nurse Ratched (a combination of wretched, ratchet and rat shit) and Billy Bibbet (rabbit, baby's bib) from *One Flew over the Cuckoo's Nest*.

 Snapshot

Write down the name of the cast – or intended cast – of your novel. Beside each name, list the resonances the names bring to mind.

 Edit

Write a list of your least favourite names. Now take a piece of your writing or a passage from a book and replace all the characters' names with ones from this black list. How does this make you feel about the characters and their actions?

THE TITLE

The most important name in the book is the title. Sometimes authors begin with the title and work their way towards it, sometimes the book is written and they are still groping for what to call it. There may be no advantage either way; however, delaying it until the book is finished is a little like calling a child 'Hey you' until it's two years old. A name is not just a facility to help us refer to things: names have layer upon layer of meaning, and they confer dignity. Search out names, both for your book and your characters. Don't force anything, but neither leave it to the last.

 David Lodge

'The title of a novel is part of the text – the first part of it, in fact, that we encounter – and therefore has considerable power to attract and condition the reader's attention.'

There is no copyright on the title of a book, so you can choose any name you want. It's worth checking, however, with *Books in Print* to see if anyone has got there before you. I think Colin Wilson erred in naming his book *The Outsider*: Albert Camus had so famously made the title his own (though admittedly called *L'Étranger* in its original French) that only confusion in the public's mind could ensue.

Occasionally a publisher will want you to change the title. Be amenable: publishers probably know what they are doing. However, if you really believe in it, stick to your guns. It is only through author intransigence that such wonders as *V* and *By Grand Central Station I Sat Down and Wept* come into existence. Although the reviewers, and sometimes your publishers too, will misquote the title, at least you have named your baby the way you wanted.

Key idea

The title of a book is the first part of its text.

Snapshot

If you haven't decided the title of a work in progress, brainstorm some options and try them out on people. Ask what the title makes them think about, what kind of story it suggests.

JOBS

The first question most people ask on meeting a stranger at a party is their name. The second is their occupation. What they do for a living, the way they spend our day, their social status – these are all important indicators of the type of person we are being introduced to.

Nothing is by chance in fiction; however, jobs of your characters have a high degree of significance. If your heroine is a waitress, you are not just saying she is poorly paid, but that she is also a servant; if she is a judge, she is not only a well-paid professional, but the implication is one of trustworthiness and judiciousness. Of course, you may use this to trick the reader: a judge called Prudence Bold may in fact be a perjuring and corrupt hypocrite. Again, use this cautiously (you couldn't really have a judge called Prudence Bold – it is too obvious).

IMAGERY

There is a point where symbolism merges into imagery, that is, the painting of pictures with words. When this happens we have to leave logic behind and feel our way aesthetically. D. H. Lawrence was a master of powerful imagery – industrial towns, galloping horses, wrestling men. In *Lady Chatterley's Lover*, the high-class mistress falls in love with a gamekeeper, a man not just of a different class but one with dirt under his fingernails. Is this symbolic, or just a wonderful picture? The fact that her husband, Clifford Chatterley, had been crippled (and made impotent) in the Great War, fighting on behalf of the industrial-military complex is significant, but it doesn't matter whether it is a symbol or not. Mellors, the gamekeeper, is his opposite: proletarian, agrarian and potent. There is no doubt what Lawrence is telling us about the bigger picture: the modern age is emasculating men.

The wonderful lie which was published under the title *Lady Chatterley's Lover* is a work of art, and it has a truth beyond documentary; an aesthetic truth which can be expressed only through symbols and metaphors.

 Key idea

Imagery is painting pictures with words.

Workshop

When you have read through this chapter, and tried some of the exercises, read back over your novel-in-progress and answer the following questions:

- Are there any unwittingly symbolic elements in your story?
- If so, are they congruent with what you want to say?
- If not, what alterations could you make to bring all elements into alignment?
- Examine your subplot. What function is it fulfilling? How could it be developed in order to contribute more to the telling of the main plot?

Next step

In this chapter we have seen how a subplot can support the main plot through resonance or contradiction. We've also seen how, when used carefully, symbolism can add extra layers to your story and deepen the experience for your readers. In the next chapter, we will be looking at character, and how to create believable people to inhabit the world you are creating.

5

Character

In his *Poetics*, Aristotle declared that the hierarchy of dramatic effects was in descending order as follows: plot, character, dialogue, music and spectacle. (The novelistic equivalent of music is perhaps style; spectacle has already been spoken of.)

E. M. Forster disagreed, considering character to be more important than plot. It was Henry James who pointed out that plot and character are one and the same.

Henry James

'What is character but the determination of incident? What is incident but the illustration of character?'

Authors tend to find their novels fall into one of two camps which they may swap between from book to book: the character-led story and the plot-led story. Characters, if they are strong enough, can evolve into pseudo-autonomous beings who are resilient enough to lead the author through the twists and turns of plot. It can be fun to travel this way, because we never know what is around the next turning. However, if as has been said, plot is the footprints of your characters in the snow, following the lead of your characters can mean a chaotic and slushy mess. It is not enough to have characters move aimlessly though a story; pattern is required, as is some sort of character change by the end of the narrative. Characters who do not learn from their experiences are most often found in the monotony of soap opera, tracing and retracing their steps until killed off by the scriptwriter.

You are less likely to be lost in a plot-led story; however, here the characters can become pegs to fit into the slots of the plot. The imposition of structure on your characters can be at the expense of what seems their realness. Although it is fanciful to say that characters take over (if they do, you had better book an appointment with your doctor), there is a fluidity and liveliness which can be gained by allowing instinct and intuition to guide your writing hand. Perhaps, as with most things, balance is the key.

Identification with the character

It is what characters *do* that makes them interesting, not just who they are. A fascinating character is made fascinating, not because of who he is, but because of what he does.

Looking into this matter further, we see that the interest in the character's actions is not so much in the action alone, but in the *anticipation* of action: *now* what are they going to do? As we explored in Chapter 2, a storyteller is in essence someone who raises interesting questions, and delays their answer. The questions, to remind you, are of two types: forwards looking (suspense) and backwards looking (mystery).

How does the magic of suspense and mystery work? How can you prevent your reader throwing the book aside in frustration, or turning to the back to find the answer? This is the challenge facing all writers: to make your reader wait for the answer, and to make the waiting enjoyable. How to do this? By coaxing the reader into caring enough about made-up people, and then putting these people in sufficiently interesting and complex situations so that the reader's sense of intrigue or compassion is activated.

The heart of this is not magnitude of action alone, nor anticipation, but identification. The reader will care what happens only if he or she cares about who it happens to, and this will happen only if the reader identifies in some way with the fictional character.

Snapshot

Analyse your own responses to the characters in a favourite novel – what is it about them that you like so much? Don't copy the characters, but do look at the techniques that made you care about them.

EMPATHY AND SYMPATHY

Identification happens through two agencies.

1 **Empathy**

Empathy is recognizing something of yourself in the character. We can empathize with any character in fiction because, as I have said, all characters in fiction are human beings, albeit sometimes in disguise. This will always be the case until the first non-human reader is found – until then fiction will always be for people, and about people.

2 **Sympathy**

Sympathy is liking what you see, that is, identifying the nice bits of yourself with the nice bits of others.

This means that your protagonist (at least) needs to be someone who is convincingly human and appealing in some way. Characters whose emotional attributes are so alien that the reader's empathy is tried, or characters who are irredeemably bad, may fail to engage because the reader is unwilling or unable to identify with them. Without this power of identification, the reader sees the characters for what they are: words on the page with no more life to them than spots of ink.

Focus point

A first-time novelist will often unwittingly base their central character on themselves. If you do this, you'll find it easy to understand the character, but you may forget to ask why other readers should care about the character.

Snapshot

Write a short description of yourself, as though you were a character in a novel. Be as brutally honest as you can.

What about the anti-heroes, the Hannibal Lecters of the fictional world? Even the anti-hero, the villain we love to hate, should have some redeeming features. These are usually power, charisma, wit, style, intelligence. For example, Hannibal is a brilliantly intelligent lover of classical music and art – and there is something in us which, against our wills perhaps, admires these qualities even in the form of a psychopathic serial killer. The character cannot be too mad, however, otherwise empathy goes out of the window.

Readers must become involved in the story, and this they do by at some level comparing what is on the page with their own experience and saying, 'Yes, that fits.' It is not the detail with which we identify, so much as the underlying humanity of the character. This is how we can weep for E.T.'s homesickness and the death of Bambi's mother – characters with whom we share no detail, but with whom we connect on an emotional level. We care about them because we recognize ourselves in them – that is empathy.

AUTHENTICITY

The underlying humanity of our characters must be authentic, whether they are humans or aliens. The reader – old, young, wise, naive – is real. The reader knows what it is to laugh, to cry, to hope; knows the inside of his or her head, and will identify only with what is true on the page. True not in terms of the facts, but in essence – what Nathaniel Hawthorne called 'the truth of the human heart'.

Pablo Picasso

'We all know that Art is not truth. Art is a lie which makes us realize the truth, at least the truth that is given us to understand.'

Making characters real

How do I make my characters real? How do I create a fictional representation of a person who is vivid, knowable, almost seeming to step off the page? Such characters are those whom readers have no difficulty identifying with, and caring for. They are characters who, for the author, seem almost autonomous, guiding the course of the plot, sometimes in surprising directions.

Real characters will be born only when the author knows them at least as well as his or her friends. This means understanding them both outside and inside. Outside knowledge means knowing their physical attributes and public persona. Inside knowledge means their more private and personal side. These two types of understanding can be called characterization and character.

CHARACTERIZATION

Characterization refers to the visible attributes and history of a person. This is often the starting point of getting to know the cast of your story. What do they look like? What is their biography? What star sign are they? What are their likes and dislikes? It is useful to write a profile of each main character in this way – listing as many attributes as you can. Their past, too: what sort of school did they go to? Do they have brothers and sisters? What sort of upbringing did they have? These are enormously important formative influences in the lives of real people. If you want to create 'real' characters, they need a personality and a history.

Characterization, though important, is often overrated by apprentice writers. If we proceed no further than listing their attributes, we can end up with nothing other than a dutiful list of adjectives and still no real live person. Although characterization is useful in giving the reader a snapshot of a person, the image that is created by surface information – the narrative equivalent of cocktail-party chat – will not linger in the mind for long. In effect, if the author supplies nothing other than this, the reader is being asked to remember a list. And lists are notoriously difficult to remember.

HOW READERS READ

It is worthwhile considering for a moment how readers read. It is natural to assume that readers have a blank space between their ears, and it is the writer's job to fill in the space with detail. However, if it were as simple as this, then everybody who read the same book would have the same detail in their head. Clearly this isn't the case – perhaps the most striking evidence of this is seeing a film of a book you have read. Sometimes the characters are just right (Bogart playing Harry in Hemingway's *To Have and Have Not* was spot-on for me); sometimes we can't believe the director's choice of casting: we see the same person in different ways. Who is right? We are both right: the purpose of fiction is not to convey facts, that is the job of non-fiction. The artist has far greater licence.

 Ursula Le Guin

'Artists are people who are not at all interested in the facts – only in the truth. You get the facts from outside. The truth you get from inside.'

The unfolding of the novel takes place in the mind of each reader, beyond the reach of the writer. Because there is an infinite variety of people, there is an infinite number of readings. The most any novelist can do is offer stimulus in the hope that the picture evoked is not too different from that intended. Giving an abundance of information can work against the process of visualization, because the more exact we want the picture to be, the more the reader has to rein in his or her imagination to fit with the facts.

Let me demonstrate. Images are conjured in the mind of readers at the speed of light. If you are deeply involved in a novel and you read: 'a young girl came into the room', you will instantly have a picture, albeit ill-defined, of a young girl. Your picture is unlikely to be the same as the author's. If you read that she has a dog beside her, a particular dog will be conjured up for you. Now if you read she is on crutches, you will probably have to adjust your picture considerably – I don't suppose you visualized that in the first place. The more information you read, the more you will have to adjust the initial picture. Take a moment to visualize the girl so far. Close your eyes for a moment and bring her to mind. Now let me add that she is wearing a blue-and-white, polka-dot dress, has white ankle socks, tiny freckles, and a big smile on her face. Oh, and she's eight years old. Starting with a picture and adjusting it again and again is hard work for the imagination. Sometimes our mind refuses to accept the data and we are blind to the fact that the character is eight years old because, in the first instance, we saw her as five.

So, what to do? We need characterization if the reader's imagination is to be guided in the right direction – we can't dispense with it altogether. I recommend you do two things. First, *be as specific as you can*, early on in the story. Thus: 'An eight-year-old girl on crutches comes into the room. A spaniel is beside her.' If you want, you can add touches at intervals throughout the story, though resist giving anything that requires an overhaul of the reader's picture.

Second, *restrict your information*. Unless the polka-dot dress is important, try leaving it out. It is the truth of the girl we are interested in, not the facts. We can dress the girl according to our impulse, let the reader have free rein unless it causes a serious misunderstanding.

Key idea

In Nigel Watt's novel *Twenty Twenty*, he didn't describe his main characters at all. Does this mean the reader would have no idea of their appearance? Not at all. William and Julia, the two main characters, are vivid and realistic for a reader. Is it a problem if one reader sees Julia as redhead, the other as blonde? No.

Edit

Take a story you have written, or a passage of the novel you are working on. Go through and eliminate any physical description of your characters. Does this change the way you see them?

Why then research your characters? What is the point of knowing their background as fully as you can? This is for your benefit, not the reader's. Doubtless you will use some of the information on the page, but most of it will lie below the surface like an iceberg. Unless you have that mass of knowledge, you won't know how they will react when you put them under pressure. In other words, you won't know their character.

Don't worry if you find you can easily visualize your subsidiary characters while your protagonist remains a blank. In real life, trying to bring a face to mind is often easier the less you know the person, while the hardest face to visualize is one's own. If, as has been said, all characters in fiction are aspects of the writer, it follows that the characters closest to oneself will be the hardest to picture. Don't worry about this: it is not the appearance which counts, but the person; not the characterization, but the character.

Write

Write a characterization list for your main cast. Cover both physical attributes and history. Include such things as: distinguishing features, style of dressing, the school they went to, siblings, type of upbringing, formative influences in childhood. You can find examples of such lists online.

CHARACTER

Far more important than the surface information is the knowledge of what sort of person your characters are. As in fiction, so in life: we make snap judgements all the time using characterization as indicators. However, it is not uncommon for us to re-evaluate this initial decision, particularly when we get to know the person. So, who is the person really? The first impression, or the person we see in action? This is the difference between characterization and character.

Robert McKee, the screenwriter, defines character simply as: 'the choices we make under pressure'. One way of viewing plot is as a narrative pressure cooker. Big or small, personal or global, conflict is at the heart of fiction. And conflict takes its toll on people. It is when people are put under pressure that they show their true colours.

One of the conventions of the disaster movie is the clash between characterization and character. The story starts with Mr Success ordering people around, but when the pressure mounts, he cracks and shows himself to be Mr Help-me-I'm-scared. The disillusioned vicar finds God, the rowing husband and wife are reunited, the wimp is a hero. True character is revealed by our critical choices, that is, the decisions we make when put under pressure.

McKee says the job of the writer is to:

- establish characterization
- reveal character
- change character for good or bad.

The novel, remember, is a journey. It is not enough to test the resources of your characters if they remain the same people at the end of the story. If this is the case, it is a journey which takes the reader nowhere. And, as I said in Chapter 2, the change in the person (that is, the 'reversal') at the end of the story need not be in the outside world.

Seven tools to convey characters

1 Physical description
2 Narrator's statement
3 Action
4 Association
5 Revelation of the character's thoughts
6 Speech
7 Others' thoughts or comments

The eight-year-old girl hobbled into the room on bamboo crutches. The look on her face was that of someone trying to hide disappointment. The old spaniel beside her looked up with rheumy eyes and she crouched to hug it to her chest. The tiny silver crucifix around her neck swung between them. It's my birthday, Jojo, she thought bitterly, and I want to go home.

'I miss mama and papa,' she lisped.

Voices came from the hallway. 'I doubt if children in Vietnam celebrate birthdays,' somebody said.

'Aren't they all Buddhists?'

1 PHYSICAL DESCRIPTION

'The eight-year-old girl hobbled into the room on bamboo crutches.' Physical description is perhaps the most obvious resource. It is not the *quantity* of detail that has effect, as we have seen, but the *quality*. I chose to tell you about the bamboo crutches rather than the blue-and-white polka-dot dress because it is more unusual, perhaps the first detail I would notice if I was an observer.

The main advantage of physical description is its concision – you can say a lot in a little space. The disadvantage is that it is passive. Drama is firstly about action. Anything passive comes second. It is, therefore, useful to feed in your description with the action, rather than giving it all at once. Thus I kept her lisp back for a few sentences.

 Key idea

> The Victorian convention of devoting several paragraphs to providing a characterization has its appeal; however, the modern reader often has limited patience. It is the story that he or she wants, and this means action.

2 NARRATOR'S STATEMENT

'The look on her face was that of someone trying to hide disappointment' is the narrator's statement. The character of the girl is building: she is disappointed, and perhaps older than her years in her attempts to hide her feelings.

3 ACTION

'She crouched to hug it to her chest' is the third resource you have – action. Physical action is vivid in a way that passive description often fails to be. Particularly if the action is the climax of a critical choice (and this *is* a critical choice for the child – she is under significant pressure), it can say more than any amount of explanation.

4 ASSOCIATION

This is more subtle: it relates to the setting and the physical detail of the situation and what it implies about the character. A film star leaving a nightclub in the dazzle of paparazzi flash bulbs is associated with success and fame. Jesus riding into town on an ass has the implication of humility. The clause 'the tiny silver crucifix around her neck' is descriptive – we assume she is a Christian, but also associative, particularly in conjunction with the rheumy-eyed spaniel. The girl is meek, perhaps spiritual in some way.

5 REVELATION OF THE CHARACTER'S THOUGHTS

This has a particular value: people may lie to each other, but they don't lie to themselves – at least, not consciously. 'It's my birthday ... and I want to go home' confirms that she is disappointed, and it reveals the reason for it.

6 SPEECH

Speech likewise reveals a lot. 'I miss mama and papa' gives us more characterization. Dialogue will be covered in detail in Chapter 6.

7 OTHERS' THOUGHTS OR COMMENTS

These give a different perspective, particularly useful if there is a discordance between the character's worldview and others' worldview. 'I doubt if children in Vietnam...' not only tells us where she is from, but also contributes to the reasons why she should feel so lonely: not only is she alone in a foreign country, but nobody understands her.

Snapshot

Choose a character from the story you are currently developing. Try to write a short paragraph introducing them that uses all seven points detailed above.

Motivation

You will only know your characters when you know how they will react under pressure. You will know how they will react under pressure only when you know their motivation. What do they want? To save their own skin? To be liked? To get the girl? Everybody wants something in fiction: conflict arises when the things are mutually incompatible, or are not forthcoming.

There is often dramatic mileage in the clash between public and private motivations. When we are under pressure it is our private, undeclared motivation that is often revealed; if this is shown to be at variance with the declared motivation, then you have dramatic interest. A character without a degree of internal conflict is likely to be flat and uninteresting. The critical choices characters make won't really plumb their depths, for they won't have any.

When you know what your character wants, you know, more importantly, what they don't want. This is invaluable to you in your role as obstacle-erector, because it means you can invent appropriate hurdles for them. If your protagonist wants to get rich, you rob her. If she wants security, you make her lose her job.

Focus point

An extreme example of a thing which is not wanted is a phobia, something George Orwell used to great effect in *Nineteen Eighty-Four*, when he invented Room 101 – a room full of rats for his rat-phobic protagonist to suffer in.

Write

It is particularly at moments of stress (that is, when plot events are stacked up against a person, forcing them to make a critical choice) that we see a character's depth. Taking the following examples, write a character study for each in 300 words. Use at least three of the 'seven tools' given earlier in this chapter.

- An old woman is opening a letter from her son. He is suggesting she moves into a home for old people. She doesn't want to go.
- A businessman is late for work. He is stuck in a traffic jam.
- A young girl is driving a horse and cart late at night through rural lanes. She falls asleep and wakes with a start: the lamp has gone out and there has been an accident – the family horse has been killed by the shaft of another carriage.

(To see what Thomas Hardy does with the last of these examples, read Chapter 4 of *Tess of the d'Urbervilles*.)

Representation

Characters in fiction are a work of art, a representation of a human being. To do justice to the full complexity of a real human being would mean writing an infinitely long book – even longer than Proust's *Remembrance of Things Past*. Unlike real people, fictional characters should be fully coherent (though possibly contradictory) and knowable in a way a real person is not. If you endow a character with more than one dominant trait, you may find your story fails in one of its tasks: to make the incomprehensible comprehensible. Readers don't want caricatures, but they do want characters of whom they can make sense.

Presenting your characters as too lifelike has another disadvantage: oddly enough, they seem less real. It is like sending actors on to stage without make-up. Far from appearing natural, they will seem pale and ghostly. People in novels are drawn with stronger lines, coloured with richer pigments than they are in real life. They react more violently, have more convictions and fewer contradictions than most real people. They are not real people at all – they are fictional conventions.

There is a balance to be sought here. Colouring your characters with richer pigments does not mean being heavy-handed with make-up. Subtlety counts for a lot: less *can* be more at times. Too much of a good thing can turn your characters into an archetype (a typical example) or a stereotype (an oversimplified example).

ARCHETYPES AND STEREOTYPES

Archetypal characters are typical examples of a certain sort of person. Seen most often in myth or allegory, an archetype has a symbolic dimension which can be used to a good effect in fiction. If you want to indicate that your novel has a deeper significance than its surface detail, that the individual character is in fact a sign of society and the world, then an archetype may be useful. An archetypical character seems to stand head and shoulders above (or below) mere mortals, for instance Allie Fox in Paul Theroux's *The Mosquito Coast* who at times exhibits almost superhuman abilities. Archetypes can erode the sense of reality you may be wanting to build in the story, an effect you may not always want to achieve. Because of this, archetypes are most often seen as minor characters.

A stereotype has all of the disadvantages and none of the advantages of an archetype. A stereotype is an oversimplified example of a certain sort of character whose representation is not only shallow, but seems to have a flashing sign advertising it. They are flat characters, with no more depth than a sheet of paper.

 Snapshot

Write a short description of the most stereotypical character you can imagine. Now list at least five character traits that would contradict this stereotype, then rewrite your description to include them.

ROUND AND FLAT CHARACTER

There was a time when readers would have been happy with a certain amount of flat characterization, even caricatures, in the stories they read. The modern taste, however, is for roundness in fictional characters, at least for the main cast. Subsidiary characters should be flat to a degree: if they are too interesting,

the reader's eye will be drawn away from the main action and
protagonists.

E. M. Forster

*'It is a convenience for an author when he can strike with his
full force at once, and flat characters are very useful to him,
since they never need reintroducing, never run away, have
not to be watched for development, and provide their own
atmosphere – little luminous discs of a pre-arranged size,
pushed hither and thither like counters across the void or
between stars; most satisfactory.'*

Charles Dickens was an author who used such flat characters to
good effect. By all means try out stereotyped characters for ironic
effect, but beware: had Dickens's main characters been stereotypes,
he would be just another unread Victorian novelist, for not only
would the cast be flat, but so too would the novel. You can get
away with flat characters if they inhabit the world of the subplot; a
stereotypical hero would be a problem. Characters provoke interest
only if they 'live' for the reader; they 'live' through the process of
identification. It is no more possible to identify with a stereotype
than with a mannequin.

If you create flat characters, you must realize they are flat. More
often than not, apprentice writers unwittingly create stereotypes,
either wholly or in part. The credibility of a round character can be
damaged if he is prone to stereotypical reactions. In either case, the
character will be a cliché: a second-hand creation, lazily constructed
and dismissive of the reader's sensibilities. Characters need grease
paint, but exaggerating their features beyond a certain point in the
hope of making them more interesting or more easily identifiable
can reduce the drama to pantomime, tragedy to farce.

Archetypes and stereotypes exist only in literature, never in life.
Human beings are never as predictable as we think they are. The
gap between expectation and result (in other words the narrative
'surprise') is the root of drama. If characters run along tramlines
deviating neither to the left nor the right, not only will they be false,

they will be boring. In fiction the gap between expectation and actuality is the source of much drama: 'will he/won't he?' has been a story since the beginning of time.

Know your characters by knowing yourself

Vivid characters are born only when the writer knows them inside out. A good novelist is at least as much a psychologist as a wordsmith, for in the end the depth and realness of your characters reflect your understanding of human beings. True understanding of people comes about when we can see the world through their eyes, and feel their feelings as though they are our own. This quality of empathy is fundamental to the author's skill. Without it a novelist can create only flat characters. With limited empathy a novelist will have a limited range: to create only realistic characters of a certain type, namely people like the novelist.

How can we extend our range as writers, thinking ourselves inside the skin of a wide variety of characters? How could Shakespeare create Hamlet, Juliet, Lady Macbeth? Was he suffering from a multiple personality disorder? I doubt it. What he was doing was accessing the extraordinary resources available to him. Not his local library, but his *brain*.

The most complex structure in the known universe is the human brain: modern computers have hardly begun to approximate human brain functions, let alone intelligence. The human imaginative faculty is perhaps without bounds; it is certainly capable of inventing a cast of thousands. You think Shakespeare was different, that you don't have much of an imagination? Look at your dreams. You don't have dreams? I don't believe you.

Shakespeare didn't have to be mad to create King Lear, but he did have to engage with the part of himself that was a madman. Those who know of such things have said that King Lear is a convincing portrait of a psychotic breakdown. How did Shakespeare know? By visiting Bedlam, queuing up behind the other gawpers to laugh at the antics of the idiots? He may have, though I'm sure he didn't laugh. But more important than external research was the internal research, the visit to the part of him which is King Lear. And there is one part of us which can respond to everyone: madman, child, queen.

How to know your characters? Look inside: everything is there. All characters in fiction – like all characters in dreams – are parts of the writer, otherwise how could they be invented? They come from inside your head, nobody else's. *To know your characters, know yourself.*

Graham Greene

'A writer's knowledge of himself, realistic and unromantic, is like a store of energy on which he must draw for a lifetime; one volt of it properly directed will bring a character alive.'

Loving your characters

If you want to move people, you have to move yourself first. You must care about your characters in order for your readers to care about them. That means you should sympathize with them as well as empathize. You must have some sort of affection for your characters, particularly central characters, otherwise your disapproval will infect the story and your readers will be repulsed by them. Make your protagonists bad, by all means, fallible, two-faced and self-centred, but don't despise them.

If you can't bring yourself to like your characters, you must nevertheless love them. You must realize that under their characteristics, and regardless of their character, there is something else: their humanity. If you don't love them, you will always maintain a distance, and the reader will sense this.

Key idea

Create characters from within yourself, and find something to love about them.

Malcolm Bradbury

'It seems to me important that you should always love the inner experience of the story, and the characters in it, experiencing along with them; rather than using them illustratively.'

Roman à clef

Roman à clef is the convention of taking people from real life and disguising them in fiction. Strictly speaking, this reference to real life should be apparent to the reader, hence the name, a 'novel with a key', a novel containing a device for unlocking hidden meaning. An example is Aldous Huxley's novel *Point Counter Point*, in which D. H. Lawrence, among others, is disguised. However, I use the term loosely to describe any appropriation of people from real life for use in fiction. There are advantages and disadvantages for the writer in this. The advantage is having a head start on the creative process: you already know something about your characters, perhaps a great deal.

The main problem is not, as many people think, the matter of libel. Even if people recognize themselves in your book (which is rare – few people see themselves as others do), they are probably more likely to feel flattered than offended. The disadvantage of taking characters from real life is that of finding yourself restricted when it comes to using your imagination. If your fictional creation has to do something which the real person wouldn't, you may find your characters refusing to do your bidding. A certain amount of pseudo-autonomy is a good sign; however, having your characters mutiny is rarely helpful in shaping a workable plot. The author must always be the boss – perhaps subordinate to the muse, but certainly in charge of the cast.

Use people from your life, by all means, but as a starting point, not as a model to copy.

> ## Key idea
>
>
> Many of my characters begin with a germ from real life, but then I allow them to develop along their own lines. Or I amalgamate characteristics from several people into one fictional creation.

> ## E. M. Forster
>
>
> *'A useful trick is to look back upon a person with half-closed eyes, fully describing certain characteristics. A likeness isn't aimed at and couldn't be obtained, because a man's only himself amidst the particular circumstances of his life.'*

The same restrictions apply to fictionalizing your own life. If the drama demands changes to the story, and you find yourself resistant to these changes because they didn't really happen, you may find yourself between two stools: fiction and autobiography.

Life is rarely as coherent as fiction with its beginning, middle and end. Even if it is, the fact that it really happened will only contribute to its appeal if the story is extraordinary. This is sometimes hard to gauge, particularly because our individual pasts are almost by definition interesting to us. What may seem significant to us may be trivial to the reader.

Workshop

Focus on your own novel-in-progress and ask yourself the following questions about your use of character:

- Interesting characters should have some type of internal conflict – the primary level of antagonism. What inner conflict could your protagonist have?
- Idiosyncrasies and flaws help make characters more believable and often more sympathetic. What such qualities does your protagonist have?
- In what ways are your protagonist's characterization and character at odds?
- What character change, for good or bad, is in store for your main cast?
- What forces are driving your main cast?

Next step

In this chapter we've learned how vital it is to imbue your characters with an authentic underlying humanity. We've seen how to do this through use of physical description, narrator's statements, action, association, revelation of thoughts, speech and others' thoughts/comments. In the next chapter we will see how characters can be further brought to life through skilful use of dialogue.

6

Dialogue

It is tempting to think that writing dialogue is the easiest part of fiction, but not so. Every word in a novel, including the dialogue, needs to do its work, otherwise it will begin to drag.

The trick of writing good dialogue is in giving the impression of real speech without emulating it. As life usually has no plot, so most conversations have no shape. Real speech is often repetitive, tautological and full of irrelevances: just try recording a conversation and then transcribing it. The result may be realistic, but it won't pass for the convention of 'slice of life' realism – it will probably be boring and far too long.

An understandable temptation with beginners is to write a great deal of dialogue: it is often easy to do, and certainly more straightforward than the struggle most of us face with description and exposition. However, if you have too many interchanges or your speeches are too long, your reader's patience will be tested. The pleasure you find in writing dialogue must, after all, be shared by the reader in reading it. Good conversational speech may look easy, but it requires discipline and a firm editing hand.

Anthony Trollope

'The dialogue is generally the most agreeable part of a novel, but it is only so long as it tends in some way to the telling of the main story.'

Key idea

Dialogue is like a rose bush – it often improves after pruning. And pruning should always aim for a natural-looking shape, even though it is quite artificial.

Snapshot

Go eavesdropping. Get on a bus or go to a café and listen to the conversations around you. Maybe make some subtle notes. How does natural conversation compare with that from books and films?

I recommend you rewrite your dialogue until it is as brief as you can get it. This will mean making it quite unrealistically to the point. That is fine. Your readers don't want realistic speech, they want talk which spins the story along.

How to convey the sort of person who goes on and on, or talks for the sake of it? In other words, how to convey a bore? Not boringly. Do not replicate their speech, or your reader, like the targets of the bore's attention, will switch off. The paradox of the novelist is in making bores as fascinating as every other character. One way of achieving this is by showing other's reactions:

> *Jack was talking about his car again, something about the wheel trims. Jill stifled a yawn.*

Lose superfluous interactions. In a film this may go unnoticed, but on the page we are unconsciously looking for the significance of every utterance. If an interchange has no significance, we may become confused, thinking that we must be missing something.

The three functions of speech

Narrative speech should perform at least one of three functions:

1 MOVE THE STORY FORWARDS

Sometimes the quickest, most important action comes out of our mouths. From the simple request or command to the most profound confession, speech is capable of fulfilling the first task of the fiction writer: telling the story.

2 GIVE INFORMATION

The imparting of information is an unavoidable necessity. We need to give credibility to the workings of the fictional world: how people got into a certain situation; how they can get out of it; the consequences of action; and so on. The problem is that sometimes this is boring stuff which can hold up the forward movement of the story. The giving of information should, therefore, be approached with sensitivity. Sometimes there is no option but to give an entire paragraph over to exposition. Often, however, we can disguise it in the action so that, like characterization, we need not absorb it all at once.

Using dialogue for exposition is legitimate, but beware of overusing it. If your characters are too obviously a mouthpiece for your intention, you will be guilty of what is called writing 'on the nose'. This means passages which read like stage directions or a cinematic voice-over. Suddenly your readers will see the artifice rather than the art, they will remember that it is a fiction they are reading, and the spell will be broken. Dialogue used for exposition often sounds hammy:

> *'When did we first meet, Carruthers?'*
> *'Twenty years ago, old chap. The Summer of Love.'*
> *'You were driving a pink VW, and I was hitch-hiking to see my girlfriend, now my wife – Anne.'*
> *'It all comes back to me now. You were a student.'*
> *'Eng. Lit. And you were a rookie journalist on* The Milwaukee Chronicle.*'*

In cases like this it is better to cut your losses and use summary rather than pretend it is part of the drama:

> *He met Carruthers 20 years ago in the Summer of Love.*
> *He was a student of English Literature, hitch-hiking to see*
> *his girlfriend, now his wife – Anne. Carruthers, a rookie*
> *journalist of* The Milwaukee Chronicle, *gave him a lift in*
> *his pink VW.*

There is a saying among screenwriters: 'Convert exposition to ammunition.' If you can sugar the pill by imparting information in a dramatic scene, your readers will hardly notice they are being informed. Thus, the two characters above could be rowing, and amid the insults, the necessary information could be inserted.

> *'You've been saying that for twenty years!*
> *I wish you'd never stopped your stupid pink*
> *VW to give me a lift...'* (et cetera)

3 CONTRIBUTE TO CHARACTERIZATION

This function should always be fulfilled, because every word that leaves your character's mouth will help illustrate the sort of person he or she is.

Focus point

If you find that the need for every speech to be in character conflicts with one of the other functions of dialogue, then look at other ways of doing the same job. You have your own authorial voice, other characters, the speaker's thoughts and so on.

Snapshot

Using the characters from your work in process, try to write a piece of dialogue that introduces the speakers while avoiding too much exposition.

Giving the impression of real speech

As your characters have different physical and emotional characteristics, so too should they speak differently. A young man will use different vocabulary from his father; an English person and an Irish person of the same age and background will have different speech patterns and idioms; an aristocrat will not use the same language as a road sweep. Italians and French and Germans speak English in different ways; people from the north of England speak differently from their southern counterparts. It may be asking a lot, but by the end of the book your readers should hopefully be capable of recognizing the speakers without any clues other than their speech.

Real speech is often a chaotic affair involving interruptions, evasions, circumlocutions, poor grammar, bad language, silences, slang. Without exactly replicating these attributes, you need to indicate their existence. Very few people speak copybook English: your fictional creations should reflect this.

Key idea

By giving your characters speech patterns you add to the characterization, and also create the opportunity to represent change so that, for instance, a character who is normally hesitant in speech can suddenly become direct and forceful at the point of crisis.

DIALECT AND FOREIGN LANGUAGES

The transcribing of dialect, complete with misspelled words and creative punctuation can be tedious for the reader. D. H. Lawrence occasionally used a full-blown form of dialect for his Nottinghamshire characters: 'Let me be mysen, and let me feel as if tha' wor littler than me! dunna ma'e me feel sma', an' down!', says Parkin in *John Thomas and Lady Jane*. We may very well want Parkin to be himself, but too much of this and he'll be doing it on his own.

The problem with transcribing dialect is not so much the vernacular, as the spelling. If readers have to puzzle over the meaning of a word, or even if the idiosyncratic spelling is just strange, their focus will stray from the scene to the artifice. If you want to establish a vernacular speaker, you will probably find light touches are enough. If you use authentic speech patterns and local vocabulary, the occasional misspelled word will be enough to remind the reader of your character's origins. The purpose of dialogue, remember, is to give the impression of realistic speech, not to replicate it.

Focus point

If you want to represent a dialect or strong accent on the page, take the time to study the grammar associated with it – this will give a convincing flavour without having to resort to phonetic spelling.

Likewise, if your setting is in a non-English speaking country, the occasional foreign word – particularly one likely to be recognized by the average reader – is enough the remind us where we are. James Clavell's novel *Shogun* provides a good example of this.

Snapshot

Take a passage of text – it can be something you have written or a piece from any book you have handy – and try to rewrite it, phonetically, in the accent of your hometown.

SUBTEXT

People in real life tend to fudge and hesitate, saying as much with what they don't say as with the words that leave their mouths. Very often – particularly in times of conflict – the words we speak only hint at what we mean. We have rows about the washing up, when in fact we are really arguing about our marriage. Therefore, be aware of the unspoken language, the subtext of the dialogue. (I am reminded of the scene in Woody Allen's film *Annie Hall* in which subtitles revealing the true meaning of the spoken dialogue are flashed up on the screen.) If you want to make your scenes more psychologically complex and more accurately reflect the essence of real speech, be aware of the undercurrents of meaning.

Focus point

Once you've written a chunk of dialogue, look back over it and ask yourself: 'What is this conversation really about?' If there is interesting subtext, your readers will be absorbed by that and simply not notice that you've also used the dialogue to move the plot forward or to give information.

Supporting your dialogue

Meaning is not only a matter of the words we say, but the way we say them. Sometimes bald speech needs assistance:

> *'I love you,' he said from behind his newspaper.*
> *'Really?'*
> *'Yes.'*

This says a certain amount, although it doesn't tell us how seriously the man intends his words to be taken. Although speech can happily stand alone, sometimes it requires support in order to bring out its full meaning. Supporting the same words of dialogue with abstract explanation goes some way to putting flesh on the bones of meaning:

> *'I love you,' he said from behind his newspaper.*
> *'Really?'*
> *'Yes.' He really did love her.*

The most effective way of supporting your dialogue is often by giving physical clues to the meaning, for instance:

> *'I love you,' he said from behind his newspaper.*
> *'Really?'*
> *He lowered the paper and held her gaze for a second. 'Yes.'*

A picture is sometimes worth a thousand words. Using dialogue in conjunction with carefully chosen action is the simplest and most effective technique I know, making previously inert scenes come to life.

Physical action performs three functions: it helps break up the dialogue (important if you have a whole page of it); it anchors the speech in the scene (reminding us where we are and what our characters are doing); and, perhaps most importantly, contributes to characterization. The action which contributes the most is revealing action, rather than action for the sake of it. Well-chosen action will say something about your characters, hopefully identifying them as nothing else does. A woman who drums her carefully painted fingernails while waiting for someone to pick up the phone; a young man who can't meet the eyes of the person he is speaking to; the old woman who unconsciously plucks at the bedclothes while listening to the doctor – pictures, all.

Key idea

Physical action is another way of revealing subtext – the actions can either confirm the words being spoken, or contradict them.

Edit

Record two or more people talking and then transcribe it. Now rewrite it, editing it down and using supportive action. Look at both drafts: which is more interesting? Which more accurately conveys the 'truth' of the situation?

Types of speech

There are three types of speech:

1 direct
2 indirect or reported
3 interiors.

For example:

'I wish you would leave me alone, Jack.'

is direct: this is audible speech, and conventionally appears between speech marks.

Jill told Jack she wished he would leave her alone.

is indirect speech, reported as though by an onlooker.

I wish you would leave me alone, Jack, Jill thought.

is called an interior or a monologue. Here we are eavesdropping on her thoughts, although no words leave her mouth. There is no technical difficulty in the use of interiors – it is the same as direct speech, minus the speech marks. If it is unclear, you can add 'she thought' after the thought, although this is not always necessary.

The value of interiors is to give the reader another level of insight into character. For instance:

> *'Are you doing anything after work?'*
> *Jack asked, leaning across her desk.*
> *Jill tried to smile, but she could smell cigarette*
> *smoke on his breath. I wish you would*
> *leave me alone, Jack, she thought.*
> *'Not particularly,' she said, edging away.*

Write

Take the main characters from your work in progress. For each, write a series of short interior monologues that express their thoughts before, during and after the main events of your story.

'HE SAID'/'SHE SAID' AND ATTRIBUTIVE VERBS

We don't read every word on the page, but scan them, often not bothering to read the end of a sentence if we have already captured the meaning. This doesn't mean that as writers we can afford to be lax, but it does mean that there are blind spots on the page. One of those is 'he said/she said'. Don't worry if you are the type of writer who feels most comfortable attributing each piece of speech. To continue with Jack and the reluctant Jill:

'How about coming out with me?' he said.
'Well...' she said.
'We could go for a meal,' he said.
'I'm on a diet,' she said.
'How about a drink then?' he said.
'Jack?' she said.
'Yes?' he said.
'Leave me alone!' she said.

With dialogue as bald as this you might be pushing your luck a bit; however, filling in this dialogue with supportive action, few readers would notice the 'he said'/'she said' refrain.

Some writers like to leave dialogue unattributed, and this is fine if it is very clear who is speaking, as in the above example. In long interchanges, particularly if the content doesn't clearly indicate who is speaking, or if more than two people are speaking, readers may find themselves having to count back. In this case an occasional indicator would be enough.

The most common problem for the reader is not a lack of information, but a surfeit of it. If you insist on attributive verbs for each piece of speech, your reader will watch fascinated as you climb further and further out along a branch which is bound to snap. For instance:

'How about coming out with me?' Jack asked.
'Well...' Jill hesitated.
'We could go for a meal,' he proffered.
'I'm on a diet,' she lied.
'How about a drink then?' he suggested.
'Jack?' she growled.
'Yes?' he grinned.
'Leave me alone!' she snapped.

Attributive verbs have the effect of taking the eye away from the speech. In effect, we check that our reading is correct. Sometimes the attributive verb is superfluous, for example 'he suggested' after 'How about a drink then?' is a waste of a reader's attention (a minor point perhaps, but that's what a novel is – a collection of minor points). Sometimes detail corrals our imagination in unnecessary ways: you might have trouble imagining Jill growling 'Jack': in your mind she might have groaned it, in which case you would have to adjust your interpretation when you read 'growled'. Sometimes in your quest for variety of attributive verbs, you will get plain silly and find yourself using archaisms such as 'expostulated', 'ejaculated', 'exclaimed', 'cried', when you just mean 'said'.

The only time an attributive verb pulls its weight is when the meaning or delivery of the spoken words isn't clear from the words themselves. For instance, in the above example 'she lied' is necessary for us to fully understand her intent.

OUTER AND INNER EARS

In order to test your dialogue, try speaking it aloud – or, better still, have someone else read it to you, preferably someone who isn't a consummate actor. If the reader wrestles with the syntax or the idiom, take note. Just because it comes out easily in the writing doesn't mean it reads well.

Robert Louis Stevenson

'Each phrase of each sentence, like an air or a recitative in music, should be so artfully compounded out of long and short, out of accented and unaccented, as to gratify the sensual ear. And of this the ear is the sole judge. It is impossible to lay down laws.'

Although reading aloud can be of help, it is the inner ear rather than the 'sensual' one which must have the casting vote. Few readers will read your dialogue aloud; in the end it must work in the silence of their mind or not at all.

Conventions of written speech

There are no rules for the layout of speech: writers from James Joyce to Malcolm Bradbury have used their own form. However, the modern convention is:

- use single speech marks
- a new paragraph is required every time a new speaker talks, even if it is just one word
- any action associated with the speaker which immediately precedes or follows them speaking is in the same paragraph.

Write

Write a scene of people disagreeing with each other, in 300 words and using mainly dialogue. If you have a novel in progress, use the characters from the story (even if the scene is to be abandoned in the final draft). If you have nothing to get you going, try one of the following:

- Some money has gone missing at a bank. The manager is interviewing all the clerks one by one in his office. Although holding back from an explicit accusation, the manager suspects one person in particular. The clerk is defensive and indignant, but also intimidated by the manager.
- There has been a three-way collision between cars on the road. One person is clearly at fault and denying it. Another person is unsure whose fault it is, but just to make sure, blames somebody else. The third person is innocent, but shaken by the accident.
- A young couple are having a first date in a restaurant. They are trying not to spoil the evening, but they disagree about everything they talk about.

Workshop

Look at your dialogue either in the above exercise, or in your novel in progress, and ask yourself the following questions:

- Do the characters speak distinctly, using their own vocabulary and speech patterns, or do they all speak in the same way?
- Underline any attributive words you've used. Are they necessary?
- Would the addition of supporting action help bring your dialogue 'to life'?
- Look for dialogue that is also exposition. Is this the best way to let your readers know what's going on? Try to rewrite the passage using a brief summary instead. Is this an improvement?
- Look at each piece of dialogue and ask yourself whether it fulfils at least one of the three purposes listed above. Does it further the story? Give information? Contribute to characterization? If it does none of these, cut it!

Next step

In this chapter we have seen how dialogue, when kept brief and significant, can move the story along, imparting information, carrying subtext and contributing to characterization. In the next chapter we will focus on viewpoint, to demonstrate that who is talking is as important as how they talk.

7

Viewpoint

A novelist is like a film director. It is not enough to say: in this scene such-and-such happens to so-and-so. If that were the case, you would produce a long synopsis, which in film is called a 'treatment', instead of a dramatic narrative. The novelist and film director must decide *how* to portray such-and-such happening to so-and-so.

Of the technical resources available to the director, the most important is the camera. The director cannot film everything from every angle – he or she must make decisions: where to place the camera; what angles to film from; what to film; what to leave out. The writer, likewise, must decide where to position the novelistic camera. This is what is meant by 'viewpoint'.

David Lodge

'The choice of the point(s) of view from which the story is told is arguably the most important single decision that the novelist has to make, for it fundamentally affects the way readers will respond, emotionally and morally, to the fictional characters and their actions.'

In a murder mystery, are you going to tell the story from the detective's viewpoint, or the suspect's or the murderer's? Or a combination of all three? Alfred Hitchcock denied us the murderer's viewpoint to famous effect in his film *Psycho*. The effect would have been very different if he hadn't done so: much of the suspense would have been dissipated, and all of the mystery. Some novels bring to the fore the significance of different perspectives. John Fowles's first novel, *The Collector*, was the story of an abduction told from two viewpoints – the kidnapper and the victim. The same story, but different camera angles.

If the viewpoint decision is the most important decision to make, it can also be the most complex. That is, unless you have proceeded intuitively, for more often than not the viewpoint decision will make itself even before the first word is written. Especially if you have a clearly defined central character and a feel for the book, there is often little hesitation.

There is a lot to be said for intuition: a novel is far too complex – infinitely so, I believe – to be fully approachable through reasoned argument. However, if you are aware of friction in the early stages of telling your story, it could be because you have chosen the wrong viewpoint. In which case it is worth a certain amount of examination of the options and their respective advantages.

Snapshot

Think of a favourite story and spend some time listing characters other than the protagonist. How might the story have changed had it been told from their viewpoint?

Before we move on to examine the types of viewpoint, it is useful to ask two questions, not that they will necessarily solve the problem, but they could point us in the right direction. The questions are: Whose story is it? What is the theme?

Whose story is it?

Is there a single hero, or more than one? If there are several, who is more important? Are they equally important? The word 'hero' is misleading here, implying qualities which the lead character may not have, for instance the unnamed narrator in Daphne du Maurier's *Rebecca* is far from heroic. But so too is the word 'protagonist' misleading, for sometimes the 'first actor' is not the main player; however, they are the main focus for the impact of the action. Thus a young child could be the protagonist of a story about his parent's divorce.

There are three types of protagonist, three options for choosing who is to be the main focus of the story. In descending order of occurrence:

THE SINGLE PROTAGONIST

This is the simplest option for the writer and reader alike. There is no difficulty identifying the hero.

> ## Key idea
>
>
>
> Readers find single protagonists most appealing for the simple reason that they identify with that character, as long as the character is sympathetic, of course.

DUAL PROTAGONISTS

This is a little trickier; you have two characters with more or less equal weight. As their author, you must decide who gets the spotlight when they are on stage together, whose action to follow when they are apart.

Focus point

With two protagonists you have ready-made cliff-hangers – once you have one in a tricky situation you change to telling your readers about the other one. This also adds to the reader's sense of time passing.

MULTIPLE PROTAGONISTS

This is the trickiest of the three. Few novelists try this because, lacking a character focus, the story itself could lack focus. Joseph Conrad used this form in *The Nigger of the* Narcissus.

If you have more than one protagonist, they should ideally be intimately connected, that is:

- be in a relationship together, or
- have their fates bound together, or
- face a common source of conflict.

In other words, though distinct in themselves, they should share a common quest. Some stories involving more than one protagonist will share all three of these, for instance *Romeo and Juliet*. If there is not a common goal it may split the book down the middle, in which case you may need to decrease the significance of one of them and turn it into a subplot.

WHAT IS THE THEME?

Theme will be explored more fully in Chapter 10. Briefly, 'theme' is the meaning behind the action – what the author is saying about the subject. For instance, if the subject is a marital breakup due to adultery, the theme could be 'Love is more important than commitment'. If this was the case, the viewpoint character is likely to be the adulterous partner. If the theme was 'Loyalty is more important than attraction', then the point of view of the cuckold may be the more obvious choice.

Types of viewpoint

In fiction there are four available options, each with its own advantages and disadvantages.

FIRST-PERSON VIEWPOINT

Sometimes called 'intense' viewpoint, this is when all the action is seen through a single 'I'. There is only one camera, as it were, and it looks through the eyes of a single person – the protagonist. This means only action that the protagonist witnesses can be reported. It is easy to hold a novel within such a tight framework – the viewpoint doesn't get out of hand because it is very simple.

The first-person viewpoint has more intrinsic dramatic focus than the other options. Because the reader lives, as it were, inside the character, this option is capable of a singleness of impact, hence 'intense' viewpoint. Because of this, it lends itself well to a very intimate treatment, which is useful if the subject is a personal, internal process.

Because the readers can know only what the protagonist knows, it is easy for the author to spring surprises on them. Suspense and tension, therefore, often work well with a first-person viewpoint.

Another advantage accrues because there is no need for the author to deliberately withhold information – what you see is what you get. (Unless the narrator is unreliable, as in Agatha Christie's *The Murder of Roger Ackroyd*, a murder mystery in which it transpires the culprit is the narrator himself. Unreliable narrators are a neat trick perhaps, but the author is open to accusations of unsporting deviousness.)

The first-person viewpoint in the most straightforward option. Having a wider focus will increase the number of decisions the author has to make: should I tell the reader what is happening in the next room, what so-and-so is thinking? The disadvantages are the opposite of the advantages. Nothing can happen without the viewpoint character knowing about it. It may be simple, but it is restrictive. If you have a very complicated story, you will have to have a lot of people coming in with messages, or an abundance of phone calls and letters.

Is it possible to have more than one first-person narrator? John Fowles succeeded with it in *The Collector*; however, it was necessary to divide the novel into parts. An ambitious thing to do – good luck if you want to try it.

If you write in the first person, and if the narrator bears even a passing similarity to you, don't be surprised if people think it's autobiographical. Proceeding in the knowledge of this might require some courage on your part!

Wally Lamb

'I like to write first-person because I like to become the character I'm writing.'

THIRD-PERSON VIEWPOINT

This is probably the most common convention: stories concerning 'he' and 'she'. There are two ways you can tell a third-person story: a single viewpoint or a multiple viewpoint.

The single viewpoint

This has the same technical advantages and disadvantages of a first-person single viewpoint; the main difference is the pronoun. The third person is perhaps less intimate, less confessional. This may be a plus if you want to avoid self-pity or self-indulgence in your protagonist. If you have a sad story to tell and you relate it from the viewpoint of the person it happened to, an unsympathetic reader could hear it as the whining of a victim. Tell the same story in the third person, and the effect may be one of pathos. The exception is if the narrator has no self-pity: a rare thing indeed. My second novel, *Billy Bayswater*, began its life in the third person. The first draft read:

> *Billy had something wrong with his brain. He touched his face in the mirror and smiled. 'Billy Bayswater brain,' he said.*

Although the work was going well, by the time a week had passed I could smell burning rubber. There was a handbrake on somewhere – I could sense the resistance. I realized that I was holding Billy at bay, not allowing myself to get too close, in part because I wanted to tell a tragic story without being maudlin. (The other part was because an intense viewpoint cuts both ways – this was going to be painful if I got too involved.) I thought I would try it in first person:

> *Billy's got summat wrong with his brain – that's what they say. I touch my face in the mirror and smile. Billy Bayswater brain.*

Suddenly the story came alive. Not only was I inside his skin, but I could use his language; and because of his lack of awareness, there was no danger of self-pity. Intimacy of this type is often central to the appeal of a novel: imagine *The Catcher in the Rye* written in the third person – I'm sure it would lose a lot.

When choosing a single viewpoint – whether first person or third person – it is important to select a character whom you can easily inhabit. In order to make the character credible and authoritative, you will need to be privy to his or her thoughts, seeing the world through your character's eyes. Although it is important to know all your main characters well, you should know your viewpoint character inside out.

Key idea

You don't need to share the same gender or history as your characters. My first novel was written through the eyes of a woman, my second through the eyes of an adolescent epileptic; however, you should be capable of imagining yourself within their skin.

Snapshot

Try to imagine a character who is your opposite in as many ways as possible. Then write a paragraph or two from their viewpoint.

The third-person multiple viewpoint

This is when the film director, as it were, has more than one camera at his or her disposal. Now the director can film anything: events happening in different locations, even if they happen at the same time. However, now the director needs to hire a good editor, for important decisions need to be made about whose viewpoint to follow.

To use multiple viewpoint well requires discipline. Having open season can be disorienting for the reader. Look at the following passage, for instance:

As he opened the door he glanced at his wife. Oh hell, he thought when he saw her face. I'm in trouble again. 'Good morning, darling,' he smiled. She might forgive me if I'm nice to her, he thought.

She said nothing, just watched him as he crossed the kitchen. He was unsteady on his feet and caught his thigh on the corner of the table. She saw his jaw tighten. It must have hurt, but he kept quiet. He feels guilty, she thought. Good.

He could feel her disapproving glare like a sunlamp on his back as he poured out his coffee. Nice and strong, he put in extra sugar to clear his hangover. He had ten minutes to get to work. Please God, don't let her row with me.

She listened to the clinking of the spoon against the china mug. She didn't know whether she hated him or just despised him. He had promised to be home early. Promised.

The viewpoint here goes: husband, wife, husband, wife. If you bat viewpoint backwards and forwards like a ball, the reader gets dizzy. We would rather live in one head at a time, guessing, if necessary, what the other person is thinking. It is best to decide whose scene it is going to be, and then stick to your decision. Again, this may be an intuitive decision, but if you are still unsure, look at the point of the scene. In this case, which is more important to convey – the husband's guilty feelings or the wife's anger?

If the scene is long, you can get away with swapping once, or, if one of the characters exits, transfer the point of view to the other. Here, for instance, we could have focused on the husband as he burns his mouth on his coffee in his hurry to leave, and then paid attention to the wife as she sits at the table thinking things over.

Snapshot

Rewrite the scene above, first from the wife's perspective only, then from the husband's, then with a single switch of viewpoint halfway through. How do you feel this affects the piece?

A straightforward way to combine viewpoints is chapter by chapter, which is what Mario Puzo did in *The Godfather*. The change of viewpoint will still be noticed, but the join between them will be legitimized by the gear change of a fresh chapter.

If you choose multiple viewpoints, limit the numbers you afford it to, perhaps just the protagonist and one or two others. If you include minor characters – the taxi driver, the waiter, the woman on the bus – you could lose focus to such an extent that the story becomes fuzzy. There is only a certain amount of room on the stage (to change my image to a theatrical one): having actors jostling for attention will seem chaotic.

The advantage of shifting viewpoint is an expanded panoramic vision. This is fine, but only as long as the author isn't caught at it. If the reader notices the shift in viewpoint or, even worse, is confused about who 'you' refers to (the second-person 'you' is called a 'shifter' in linguistics; that is, a designation which changes according to who the speaker is), awareness of the author will intrude in the reading process. This is like the moment in a bad film (back to my original image) when the boom microphone bobs into view. Such reflexiveness can be intentional, in which case we are in the realm of metafiction, that is, fiction about fiction. But that is straying far from the classic novel which is the subject of this book.

GOD'S-EYE VIEW

This is multiple viewpoint taken as far as it can go. A truly omniscient viewpoint hovers above the story, the reader listening in to characters' thoughts like a telepathic eavesdropper. The advantage is manifest: nothing is hidden, the fictional world is laid out in front of us like a map.

In some novels the divine status is less exalted, and we have a sort of demi-god's-eye view where the deity makes occasional visits to the lower worlds, appearing in the guise of a narrator in a single-viewpoint story. For instance, a chapter could begin like this:

The early-morning sun shone as brightly and as sweetly as a Disney cartoon on Peewee's house. The white slats of the picket fence against the perfect green of the lawn was a picture to behold. A blackbird bobbed its tail and opened its throat to sing. The postman, a parcel under his arm, whistled happily as he knocked on the front door.

and then move on to a single viewpoint in the next paragraph:

Peewee heard the postman's knock and sat up straight. Today's the day, he thought. He leapt from his bed and banged on the window frame to open it, but it was stuck. He could see the postman by the front door. 'I'm here,' he called. 'Yoo-hoo.' He banged harder on the frame and heard the pane crack.

continuing with the single viewpoint unless or until the narrator is needed again.

The disadvantage of a god's-eye view is significant: the reader, like the narrator, can float above the scene, passing through walls like a ghost, never really getting involved. If your intention is to produce a cool, perhaps ironic tone, this distance may be in your favour. If you have an emotional tale to tell, you may find the effect is the opposite of intense.

 Focus point

Most of the great nineteenth-century novels were written from the god's-eye viewpoint, so if you choose it you run the risk of appearing a little dated. On the other hand, it's a simple way to create a period feel.

Write

Relate one of the following scenes in 300 words, first from one viewpoint, and then from another:

- The first day at school. A young teacher, fresh from college, faces his or her first class. (The viewpoint of the teacher, and then one of the pupils.)
- There has been a road crash. (Viewpoint of a bystander, and then the crash victim.)
- A young woman helps an old blind man across the road. (Viewpoint of the woman, and then the man.)

Now relate the same scene through the god's-eye view.

What tense?

Basically, there are two main options: present tense and past tense. It is more usual to tell stories in the past tense, a tradition which perhaps goes back to the days when storytellers related tales of a mythical past.

The advantage the present tense has over the past tense is in giving a sense of immediacy. When I changed viewpoint in *Billy Bayswater*, I also changed the tense from past to present, with the intention of increasing the closeness between the reader's world and Billy's.

Edit

Take a piece of your own writing and rewrite it in:

- a different viewpoint
- a different tense.

The impact of viewpoint decisions

The only rule about the use of viewpoint and tense is that there is no rule. If a particular technique works, use it. Some successful novelists are cavalier with viewpoint, dealing it out like a pack of playing

107

cards; some remain with a single focus. It is important to realize there is nothing inferior about using the single viewpoint: a simple form is not an inferior form. Nor does a sophisticated treatment or use of tenses ensure a good book. In the end, everything should be justifiable in terms of plot, because, otherwise, why do it?

This is complicated stuff, and is where reading plenty of fiction can be useful. Read critically, seeing how the author uses technique, and what effect is achieved.

Compare the impact of these scenes, both describing parents leaving a young son at boarding school. The first is from *The Prodigy*, Herman Hesse's second novel:

> *When the time came round for the boys to say goodbye to their mothers and fathers, it was a much sadder business. Some on foot, some by coach, some in any kind of transport they had been able to find in their haste were now disappearing from the view of their abandoned offspring and continued to wave their handkerchiefs for a long time in the mild September air until the forest finally swallowed up the travellers and their sons returned quiet and thoughtful to the monastery.*

This is a third-person adult's viewpoint (in fact, a god's-eye view). James Joyce's second novel, *A Portrait of the Artist as a Young Man*, published nine years later, deals with a similar scene in this way:

> *The first day in the hall of the castle when she had said goodbye she had put up her veil double to her nose to kiss him: and her nose and eyes were red. But he had pretended not to see that she was going to cry. She was a nice mother but she was not so nice when she cried. And his father had given him two fiveshilling pieces for pocket money. And his father had told him if he wanted anything to write home to him and, whatever he did, never peach on a fellow.*

Joyce takes the child's viewpoint, focusing on the details that a child would. What impact does this have? Suddenly the tripod of our figurative camera is lowered: we see the world from the level of a child while Herman Hesse's camera is on the top of a crane. With Joyce, we have a human scale (and, importantly, a *small* human's scale), in the Hesse example, a more considered, philosophical attitude. Which is more effective? Though critical theory is never more than a matter of opinion, I consider that the passage from Joyce is both stronger and weaker than Hesse's. Stronger, because if our protagonist is a youngster, viewing the world as an adult reduces some of the vividness of the telling. The detail Joyce chooses to give us (the red nose and pocket money) contributes more to the creation of a live character than Hesse's focusing on modes of transport.

Herman Hesse, however, has the advantage of using the more simple, and therefore more forceful, tense. While Hesse says 'When the time came round...', Joyce, to be consistent would have said 'When the time *had come* round...' While Joyce says 'when she *had said* goodbye she *had put* up her veil', Hesse would have said 'when she said goodbye she put up her veil.' Does this quibbling about tenses show an unnecessary pickiness towards the work of a great master? Perhaps. However, it is my opinion we should lose all superfluous words, streamlining our prose so the readers forget they are deciphering a semiotic convention. We have to somehow condition the reader's synapses so the words on the page seem as though they have come from the reader's head, not ours.

Snapshot

Take a passage from a favourite novel and rewrite it, changing viewpoint and tense. Assess the impact of the change.

Tone

As well as viewpoint, there is something we can call 'tone', that is, the quality of language the writer uses. This, in its own way, has as much impact on the reader's experience as does viewpoint. To return to the image of the film director with a camera, the choice of tone is akin to the choice of filter on the lens and how the scene is lit. Is the picture to be distorted? Softened round the edges? Shown starkly, under a bright light? Although there are no clear distinctions between soft and stark, straight and distorted, there are obvious extremes of tone which, as E. M. Forster suggested, we can call Impersonal and Personal. Impersonal language is more formal, and remains largely uncoloured by the viewpoint character, while the Personal tone is more conversational, using the vocabulary and idiom of speech.

A second advantage of Joyce choosing the child's viewpoint is the privileged personal tone it allows him to use. A sentence such as 'She was a nice mother but she was not so nice when she cried' would have been incongruous and twee had we not been seeing the action through the eyes of a child. As it is, it contributes to our inhabiting the mind of a child – clearly Joyce's intention.

 Write

Write a short 'first day at school' scene, first from the viewpoint of the child, then the mother, then the father.

Taken to the extreme, the personal tone can become a so-called 'stream of consciousness', a style of writing that James Joyce also used to famous effect. Compare these scenes set in graveyards; the first is from my novel *The Life Game*:

> *It was late August and the Atlantic wind flattened the uncut couch grass on the bare hillside. It was a bleak spot for a graveyard, on an exposed slope facing the reek, a triangle of Clew Bay visible in the tuck between two mountains. There was no church or building of any sort, just a drystone wall to keep the sheep out and the incongruous tombstones like granite outcrops... Kate wandered through the graveyard while Michael tidied up his wife's grave. Brushing aside the weeds and scraping off the moss she read the inscriptions. Here lies the body of Patrick McGuinn; Pray for the soul of Mary Grady.*

The second extract is from James Joyce's *Ulysses*:

> *Mr Bloom walked unheeded along his grove by saddened angels, crosses, broken pillars, family vaults, stone hopes praying with upcast eyes, old Ireland's hearts and hands.*

More sensible to spend the money on some charity for the living. Pray for the repose of the soul of. Does anybody really? Plant him and have done with him. Like down a coalshoot. Then lump them together to save time. All soul's day. Twentyseventh I'll be at his grave. Ten shillings for the gardener. He keeps it free of weeds.

Both scenes are similarly related in the third person, past tense. The tones, however, are very different. There is no intrinsic advantage in being either personal or impersonal, the success of a tone depending, as it does, on its appropriateness to what the author is trying to do. The fashion of contemporary literature – perhaps all culture – is towards the informal; the modern novelist, certainly, is less distant, more of a buddy and less of a tutor than in formal times. But why do some novelists choose a highly personal tone? The most compelling reason is because using the language of the protagonist, particularly one who holds nothing back from readers, means we can be more intimate with them. An impersonal tone will hold the reader at bay, which indeed, may be an advantage if pathos or irony is intended.

There is no right and wrong in this, just a matter of choosing the most effective tools for the job. Perhaps as novelists we need to feel our way into these questions, allowing our narrative decisions to make themselves. Perhaps we should examine our choices only if we suspect we're using a hammer when a screwdriver would be better.

Workshop

Getting the viewpoint right is vitally important. The decision is often made instinctively, so it's worth asking yourself some questions about your choices before you get too far ahead with your novel.

Ask yourself 'Whose story is this?' Play devil's advocate – what if the protagonist isn't who you thought it was? Play around, experiment, rewrite parts of your book from the viewpoint of the antagonist, a minor character, even an animal. Even if you decide to stick with your initial decision, you might find out some interesting things about your story.

Look back over things you have written in the past – short stories, aborted novels, even the exercises you have completed while working through this book. Do you instinctively write in first person? Third? Are you often a God-like, omniscient narrator? If you find that you tend to favour one perspective, try experimenting with others. Don't worry if you prefer your original choices. Sometimes the way you write naturally is the way you write best.

Is your novel written from a single viewpoint? Get a trusted friend to read your work in progress, then ask them if there's anyone else in the story they would like to hear from, a character who might shed a new and revealing light on the events that take place. Sometimes a fascinating new viewpoint can be hiding in plain sight.

Do you favour the past or present tense in your writing? If your novel is written in past tense, pick a particularly dramatic or action-packed scene and try rewriting it in the present tense. Does this add a sense of immediacy?

Spend some time thinking about tone. What is the tone of your favourite books? Can you pinpoint it? Write a paragraph describing the tone you would like to achieve in your novel. Read through your work and highlight any language you feel that suits this tone. Use a different colour to highlight any language that contradicts it. Ask yourself – does my language need to be more 'personal'? Or would the tone I am trying to achieve benefit from a more detached, impersonal tone? You can play around with your work as much as you want. No change needs to be permanent, but sometimes experiments lead to epiphanies.

Next step

In this chapter we have seen how viewpoint, tense and tone can be intrinsic to a novel's success, and how experimenting can allow you to see your work in a whole new light. In the next chapter we will look at setting the scene and building a sense of place through your writing.

8

Setting the scene

Characters and their actions need to be anchored in some sort of physical reality, otherwise they will lack a sense of substance. In our fascination and excitement for the unfolding drama, we may underestimate the importance of setting.

Sometimes a sense of place will be so subtle as not to be noticed; sometimes it will dominate the story, for instance Egdon Heath in Hardy's *The Return of the Native*, or the labour camp in Solzhenitsyn's *One Day in the Life of Ivan Denisovitch*, or the pink house in Styron's *Sophie's Choice*. But whether to the fore or not, a place should have a character as much as any of the cast. And like human characters, it has the same requirements of realness: a sense of three dimensions, credibility, and the feeling that the author is speaking from experience.

Key idea

The setting of a novel is like the flour in a cake: perhaps less compelling than the nuts and dried fruit, but if you forget to include flour in the recipe, you'll have no cake.

Researching the setting

Robert Louis Stevenson

'The author must know his countryside, whether real or imagined, like his hand.'

If your setting is familiar to you, there is the advantage that you won't have much research to do. If you don't know the physical world of your story, you need to get to know it. Real places can be visited, or if that's not possible, read about. Use any resource you can: watch movies which were filmed there, talk to people who know the setting well, read guidebooks, study street plans. Use the Internet to find out factual information and to track down people's accounts of places and experiences that you are interested in. You can set up Google Alerts on topics that interest you, and you will then be emailed every time they come up on the web. Google Street View lets you take a virtual stroll down almost any street in the world.

If you can go there, don't just look at the big picture, but notice the small things: smells, the type of litter, the look of the people who live there. If it is a building, notice the quality of the light, how the floorboards squeak underfoot or the strip light in the kitchen buzzes. If it is a foreign country, absorb as much of it as you can: the quality of the banknotes (in Pakistan they are often so old, they are as soft as cloth), how people drink their tea (quarter of an inch of sugar in the bottom in Turkey, and the spoon still in the glass) the telephone dialling tones, the taste of the water and quality of plumbing. It is the small things which can make all the difference in evoking the atmosphere of a place.

If your setting is imaginary, you need to be able to answer exactly the same sorts of questions. Just as you will be able to fully know your characters only when you have fully imagined them, so too must you know the place well enough in order to answer *any* question about it. Not that you will have the information to hand, but that, if necessary, your intuition will supply it. The research in this case is internal – you must let your imagination go to work. The advantage? Cheap on the pocket and because the place is not real, nobody can contradict you. The disadvantage? If your imagining is not thorough, it won't seem real anyway.

Focus point

In an imaginary setting, don't make things too convenient. Not every village has a pub, not every urban street has a bus stop nearby. Build in some imperfections to create a sense of reality.

Snapshot

Spend half an hour browsing on Google Earth or Street View. Find a couple of places that interest you and write a short yet evocative description.

Once again, there is a difference between information and truth. A certain veracity is needed, but the essence of a setting is far more important. A reader who doesn't know the setting will probably take your word for the information, and unless you make a significant blunder, those who do know it will fill in the missing bits without being aware of it. However, if you fail to capture the truth of a place, both types of reader will sense something amiss.

Ernest Hemingway

'A writer, if he is any good, does not describe. He invents or makes out of knowledge personal and impersonal and sometimes he seems to have unexplained knowledge which could come from forgotten racial or family experience.'

The reader should have no trouble seeing the backdrop behind the action. Whether actual or imagined, in order to effectively communicate this sense of place requires the author to view it outside in. This means seeing it as the reader might, particularly someone for whom the setting is unfamiliar. See it freshly, without prejudice or a dull eye: this advice holds true for all physical description, whether of people or places. Your setting doesn't have to be magnificent or exotic – it could be a council house, or an office – but it should be *special*. It should have a presence to it.

 Key idea

Powerful artists are those who often show us familiar things in unfamiliar ways, helping us see through our self-imposed blinkers to the specialness, the uniqueness of the place.

 João Guimarães Rosa

'*The novelist's job is to reveal and unfold, not simply portray. The novelist works with the things that pass unobserved by others, captures them in motion, brings them out into the open.*'

Choosing your setting

Sometimes your setting will choose itself. If this is the case, don't resist the pull, that is, unless the choice of location stretches the reader's credibility. If you are casting around for a suitable setting, consider what different places offer in terms of dramatic resources. I have found two things in particular of great value: isolation (not being able to run for help enables the pressure to mount), and weather (particularly extremes). Although everywhere has dramatic potential, some landscapes lend themselves more than others to fictionalization: isolated cottages, windswept fishing villages, big cities. Would *Wuthering Heights* have been as powerful set in a city; *The Heart of Darkness* in Surrey and not Africa?

Just for fun, take something you've written and rewrite it using a completely different setting. If the story takes place in a school, reset it on a spaceship. Be a bit outrageous. It might seem silly, but having your characters react to an unusual setting could reveal some surprising new truths about them.

Making scenes real

Experience is not an abstract matter; it is deeply rooted in our physicality. When we think of a place we know, we don't see 'room', 'building', 'scenery' – these are concepts. We see the flowered wallpaper, the mullion windows and varnished front door, the sweep of a hill. When we look back at events in our pasts we may label them: 'my first day at school', 'the time I fell off my bike', but if we look closer, we realize what made them real at the time, and what makes them real now is the sight and sound and feel of things. Experiences are concrete, tangible, sensory – it is only later that we conceptualize them.

Will Rogers

'People's minds are changed through observation and not through argument.'

One way of looking at the novelist's task is as a changer of minds. The change being sought may be profound, or it may be just a change from boredom to excitement, but just as the protagonist should be different by the end of the tale, so too should the reader. How to change a reader's mind? By argument, discussion, persuasion? This may have a place in the novel, but the starting point is far closer to home. The novelist must begin by painting a sufficiently vivid picture of an imaginative world which is capable of firing the reader's imagination. How to paint such a picture? The first step is making it real for yourself.

RECREATE A SCENE, DON'T DESCRIBE IT

Your reader will experience the reality of a setting only if you have experienced it for yourself, even if only in your imagination. If you are writing about your first day at school, you need to return there in your memory and see the red plastic chairs, and smell the Plasticine and gravy, and hear the sound of a boy crying for his mother. Revisiting the past may be uncomfortable, but if you want a setting with depth, you need to go into the discomfort. Recreate a scene, don't describe it. Inhabit it, don't write around it. Once you have set the scene in your own mind, *then* you can be more conceptual, talking about your feelings and the thoughts you were having. Only then will words like 'classroom', 'afraid', 'why is that boy crying?' really hit home with the reader.

What the reader is seeking to do is vicariously experience what you are evoking: excitement in a thriller; romance in a love story; tangibility in terms of the setting. If you want to communicate this experience fully, the readers will, in effect, have to sit in the red plastic chair with you. This means supplying them with sensory clues so they can make it real for themselves. As simple as that.

We can't communicate something which the readers haven't already experienced. Try describing 'blue' to a blind person. The way verbal communication works is by supplying clues which set off a process within readers, in effect reminding them of something they have already experienced. In this way, they will be able to think themselves into your skin because they will compare your experience with something similar to their own. Even if we've never sat in a red plastic chair, most of us know 'red', 'plastic' and 'chair'.

 Write

Write a scene of at least 500 words describing your first day at school. Use as many sensory clues as you can.

THE IMPORTANCE OF DETAIL

Storytelling is picture painting with words. This means authors need to keep their eyes open and convey what they see. And once conveyed, to step back, to withhold judgement. An author just gives the facts in all their specificity and concreteness – what the Zen poetess Natalie Goldberg calls 'original detail', that is, the unadorned, humble facts – and allows the readers to reach their own conclusions. Trust the power of images to evoke.

Natalie Goldberg

'Stay with what is and it will give you everything that isn't. From this wooden table I am leaning on, I can build a whole world of fiction.'

Snapshot

Pick one of the following settings and spend 15 minutes writing down as many 'original details' about it as you can.

- Your teenage bedroom
- The house of a grandparent or older relative
- Your secondary school common-room
- Your doctor's waiting room
- The garden shed

THE IMPORTANCE OF NAMES

A novelist should be omniscient. You should know your creation as a little god would – all the detail, all the depths. And the most specific way of indicating something is by naming it. So use the names of things: say 'elm', not 'tree'; 'angora', not 'wool'.

You need to be informed, so if necessary learn the names of plants and flowers, breeds of dog, tones of colour, types of cloud, brands of cigarette.

Naming helps you and the reader get a grasp of things, it helps anchor you on the page. And it tells the reader something of vital importance: that the author is authoritative. The absence of detail, the failure to name something betrays a lack of grasp of the subject. Use of detail, on the other hand, says 'I was there and it was like this.' When detail is absent, the reader senses that the author is likewise absent. When the author is removed from the page it is like speaking to someone behind a wall: we can hear the words, but they're muffled. We have to guess the expression on the speaker's face, the emphasis they are giving words. We get the gist, but the spirit is lacking.

Perception and selection

Perception is the first step: what is really happening, not what you think is happening. What is the real physical tangible reality? As the motto goes: show, don't tell. But just 'showing' isn't enough, in the same way that a film director just waving the camera blindly around isn't enough. The art is in the selecting, the editing, the discrimination. When you are describing a scene, *choose*. Focus on what is important, unique, special (everything is important, but there is a hierarchy of significance) about this person, this room, this landscape.

Focus point

There is no checklist against which to measure your decisions: *this* is what it means to be an artist – the use of aesthetic judgement to choose between what is live and what is inert.

Henry James

'The only classification of the novel I can understand is into that which has life and that which has not.'

Some objects are inexplicably 'alive', seemingly vibrating with character; others are dead, lacking energy and the ability to assert themselves on the scene. D. H. Lawrence called this quality of aliveness, 'quickness', which he gropingly defined as 'an odd sort of fluid, changing, grotesque or beautiful relatedness'. We live in a world in which objects are increasingly dead: mass-produced consumer items, synthetic material, throw-away gimmicks and junk – it is your job to sift through this to find the 'quick'.

Snapshot

Look around yourself. What objects would you call 'quick', and what 'dead'?

WHAT TO SHOW AND WHAT TO LEAVE OUT

How much information to give is often a problem at first, but once you get the hang of it, you'll probably find it easy. I find it useful to think of it as a film: what would I expect/want to see on the screen? You don't have to show everything – allow the readers to fill in the missing bits for themselves. They have an imagination as well as you.

Respect the reader's intelligence as well. There is no need to cross every 't' and dot every 'i'. The average reader can reach his or her own conclusion, deciding what is significant and what is not. If you create vivid enough scenery, your readers will move your characters around it for you, but only if you leave the readers with room for their imaginations to breathe. It's better to give too little than too much.

Key idea

Remember that your choices will have emotional and symbolic resonance. Choosing to describe the child crying for his mother or the joy of brand-new Plasticine will create quite different resonances.

VISUALIZATION

Hopefully, you are capable of visualizing the scene so vividly that you can look around in your mind's eye and select any detail you want. Don't worry if you don't have this facility at the moment – it improves with practice. It helps if you take your time: a novelist needs to take things slowly, not rush ahead.

Focus point

> If I have trouble visualizing a scene, I try again just before I fall
> asleep at night, or when I'm in the bath, or feeling drowsy in
> the afternoon.

If the imagination has stage fright, try relaxing, taking the pressure
off. We have extraordinary imaginations, and truly marvellous
abilities to evoke pictures in our minds. All of us.

Close your eyes and get as much of a picture as you can; then try
running the action as though it's a film. Once you have a picture
in mind, describe what you see – the subtle things as well as the
obvious – as simply and as accurately as you can.

When I come across passages of 'telling', I sometimes feel that the
author is struggling to picture the scene. This isn't a lack of talent
showing, just a lack of visualization. A shame, because this is the
most fun part of writing. What other job can you do with your eyes
closed and your feet up?

Seeing imaginary scenes with your eyes closed (or open, if that is
the case), and then transcribing them on to paper is a large part of
the writer's job. Why is sight so important? Because the impact of
settings in real life is largely visual (about half of the brain is given
over to visual processing, so they say). Humans are very visually
oriented, so giving visual clues to the reader is important. If we were
bats, our books would be full of sound pictures.

THE IMPORTANCE OF FOCAL LENGTH

Unless you focus your own eye well, everything might seem a blur
to the reader. Ford Madox Ford recommended seeing the action you
are describing as taking place on a brightly lit stage – everything
is available for your inspection, objects thrown into sharp relief
against each other.

Fiction is perhaps closer to film than the stage in this regard, because
the writer, like the camera operator, has three shots at his or her
disposal: the long shot, the medium shot and the close-up. If I can
extend Ford Madox Ford's metaphor, imagine you have a state-
of-the-art camera with the ability to zoom macro or micro so that

whatever is happening on the stage you can film, in whatever detail you choose, from whatever angle you choose. And all it costs is the price of a pen and paper. Writers early in their apprenticeship have a tendency to use mostly long- or mid-range lenses: we get the layout or rooms, and where people are positioned, but nothing on a more intimate scale. And the unfortunate reader has to watch the play from the cheap seats, with no opera glasses.

Snapshot

If you were a film director, which three details in your present environment would you focus on? What focal length would you use?

MAKE A SCENE OF IT

Look for the drama and interest in every scene. If there isn't any, find some. Occasionally, scenes are needed for expository purposes to fill the reader in with information. See if you can leaven such a scene with some drama – 'a thing done'. I am reminded of a scene in the Paul Hogan film *Crocodile Dundee II* which could have been dull had they not made a drama out of it: a detective visits our hero while he is having breakfast. Dundee is making toast, and offers the detective some, but then accidentally drops a piece on the floor. Dundee hesitates, and we think he will throw it away, but the man hasn't noticed, so Dundee brushes it off and then puts it on the detective's plate. The necessary but dull information the detective has come to deliver is thus made fascinating as we watch him talking while abstractedly picking pieces of grit from his mouth with every bite of toast he takes. We can do the same on the page if we have imagination and talent.

Write

Take a familiar setting – a room or a landscape – and describe it through unfamiliar eyes.

SETTING THE EMOTIONAL SCENE

The scene you are setting, of course, is not purely physical, it is also emotional. So, as well as showing us the fraying counterpane and the cobweb catching the sun, show us human reactions within this setting. Human *reactions*, not concepts. Again, 'showing not telling' is what works best. Imagine you are the film director this time, not the camera operator: how would you show 'lonely', 'depressed', 'happy'? You can't have your characters walking round with signs around their necks. You have to imagine your characters and ask yourself what exactly 'lonely' looks like on their face and in their body.

Particularly with emotional scenes (and don't forget excitement is an emotion) it pays to zoom your reader in close. And I mean close. Pupils dilating, hair bristling, palms sweating, chewing on a bottom lip, an eyelid twitching, lips parting, a raised eyebrow: tiny things which can say a lot.

However, don't overdo it. It is sometimes difficult to restrain our enthusiasm for what we are writing, and the purple ink begins to flow. Particularly when dealing with highly emotional scenes, it is worth being restrained. The reader's imagination, if primed properly, can have a hair trigger – one or two clues, and away it goes. Beware a well-intentioned but heavy-handed approach where the reader feels bludgeoned. Again, trust the power of images to evoke. Allow the readers to reach their own conclusions.

Workshop

Is your setting real or imaginary? Or maybe a combination of both? If you haven't yet settled on a setting for your novel, think about your favourite books and films. Where are they set? How do they evoke a sense of place? What draws you to these settings?

Look at any description you have written setting the scene for your novel. Does your description activate all five senses? Highlight any sensory clues you have used. Ask your trusted friend to read your work and then describe the setting to you. Does their understanding match yours?

If you are struggling with visualizing your setting, set aside half an hour and free-write about it. Keep your pen moving, write whatever comes into your head. Have you uncovered any new details?

Go through your work in progress and underline any instances where you have used a general description rather than a specific name. Look up an alternative.

You need to be ruthless about purple prose, even when you are setting the scene. Pay attention to rogue adjectives and adverbs. We'll cover this in much more detail in the next chapter.

Next step

In this chapter we have seen how the setting of your novel can become almost another character. We've learned the importance of research, visualization and sensory clues in constructing a tangible sense of place. In the next chapter, we will be building on what we have learned about the importance of language to explore the development of your own unique style.

9

Style

Style is a subject about which many experienced writers have expressed an opinion. And although voiced in different ways, they all say more or less the same thing: style is not something added to a piece of work – it *is* the work. I'm reminded of the story that the poet Benjamin Zephaniah tells of the moment in his boyhood when he became a vegetarian. His mother had served up beef burgers for tea, and – inquiring mind that he had – he asked where beef burgers came from. 'They come from cows,' his mother answered. 'And where does the cow get them from?' he asked. You can imagine his mother's expression when she had to tell him: 'They are the cow.'

Style is the expression of the writer, in the way a beef burger is an expression of the cow. Writing style is not something magicked out of nowhere, unconnected to the author; it is, as Strunk and White say, 'nondetachable'.

Key idea

Style isn't added to the work – it *is* the work.

Gustave Flaubert

'Style is life! It is the very life blood of thought!'

Find your own style

The challenge facing us as writers is in finding the perfect expression of who we are, to somehow find ourselves – what we have to say and the voice to say it – so that others can understand perfectly. How to find ourselves? *Not* by wandering round in circles. If we think we know what a writer is, if we keep our heads down and dismiss the idea of a journey of discovery, our writing will never be more than mediocre. We will have found our rut and we will follow it till kingdom come.

If we want to reach for the stars, however, we have to find ourselves. If we want to find ourselves, we have to get lost – to give up all ideas of who we are, who we think we are, who we want to be, who we think we should be.

Key idea

Being a writer is an insecure vocation, not solely for financial reasons, but because writers have to rediscover themselves every day: who am I this morning? What do I believe now? If I open my mouth, what sounds will come out?

Snapshot

One of the best ways to develop a personal style is to keep a regular diary or journal. Write as often as you can about your life and your thoughts and you will find your style evolves dramatically.

Particularly for those of us who are admiring readers, style can be a problem. If it is a quality we enjoy in others, we may long to be able to reproduce such enjoyment. Admiration, however well intentioned, can easily turn to emulation: another rut, but somebody else's in this case.

However, there is value in studying the techniques of others, just as students of painting copy the works of masters. And so, at least at first, I recommend you try out as many different writing styles as you can. Wilfully getting lost, you may discover your own style in the process. Remember, though, that copying is an *exercise*, and the point of an exercise is not to produce an end product, but to furnish us with the skills so that we can write our own story in our own way.

Snapshot

Try to rewrite a passage from your novel in the style of one of your favourite writers.

So, beware of adopting another's style as your own: there is a difference between being influenced and copying – one openly acknowledges the provenance, the other is fraudulent. Not only that, but if we adopt another's style wholesale, our writing is likely to be highly self-conscious, perhaps narcissistic. Our eye, as it were, will be on the pen in our hand rather than on our reader's face. And how will perceptive readers react to the fraud? Their instinct will tell them that something is amiss, that the author is walking in someone else's shoes.

Laurie Lee

'No writing which is self-consciously literature means much to me or means much to the reader – I think he dozes off. But if it sounds right, if it's like a voice in your ear, if it has all the rhythms and surprises of the spoken voice, you are suddenly listening to a living experience – then you know you're getting somewhere.'

DON'T TRY TOO HARD

How to get this naturalness of tone? Simple: stop trying so hard and use language which comes naturally to you. To an outsider this might seem the easiest thing in the world to do, but not so – we don't always know when we're trying too hard.

Focus point

Watch out for the signs: if you're chewing on your pencil and using your thesaurus for every other word, the chances are you're struggling to be a writer. If you rewrite the same sentence five times, if you find yourself groping for the impressive word, stop it.

Forcing yourself to produce a sound which may be against your natural inclination rarely results in anything but cacophony. Your sentences will be leaden and uninspired. The reader will sense the strain, and will be uncomfortable. You will tire easily and wonder why. No fun.

Fowlers' preferences

Although there are no rules for good writing style, there are what the Fowler brothers call 'preferences': principles from which to start and only stray from with good reason. They list five in *The King's English*:

1 PREFER THE FAMILIAR WORD TO THE FAR-FETCHED

Don't say 'digitigrade' when you mean 'tiptoe'. If your intention is to communicate, use words the average reader should understand without recourse to a dictionary. We may love the sound of particular words, we may love to show off our own erudition; you must remember that this love may not be shared. Usually, the only person impressed by our learning is ourselves.

Have a look over your work. Are there any unnecessarily 'fancy' words in there? Try replacing them with their simpler equivalents. Read through again – is this an improvement?

2 PREFER THE SINGLE WORD TO THE CIRCUMLOCUTION

'Circumlocution' means speaking in a roundabout way: valuable in dialogue if it contributes to characterization, but tedious in non-dialogue. Accuracy and concision are valuable skills to have if you want to hold the reader's attention. Sloppy writing may indicate sloppy thinking, and perceptive readers may consider they are wasting their time.

Tautology is a close cousin of circumlocution: this is saying the same thing, in effect, twice. Writing 'He crossed *to the other side of* the road' may not be a heinous crime, but enough of these and the text will have an ill-defined bagginess. Brevity has a lot to do with good style. Like a suit that has been badly cut, extra material can ruin the way a sentence hangs.

3 PREFER THE SAXON TO THE ROMANCE

Saxon words are those which most commonly feature in colloquial speech. Romance words are those whose roots are Latin. Many writers, under the illusion that literary language equals formal language, write in a way they would rarely speak (with the exception of policemen who 'proceed' instead of 'walk', 'observe' instead of 'see', 'caution' instead of 'warn'). Modern readers are far more informal than their Victorian ancestors: talk to them as you would to friends.

4 PREFER THE SHORT WORD TO THE LONG

That is, unless a long word is better.

Stendhal

'I know of only one rule: style cannot be too clear, too simple.'

5 PREFER THE CONCRETE TO THE ABSTRACT

This is the most important of the five preferences. Physical senses, because they are all more or less shared by people, are less of a problem than concepts, which by definition are abstract.

 Key idea

If you were good at English at school, you may have enjoyed seeking out new words. If you were bad at English, you may feel that your vocabulary isn't good enough. In both cases, forget about it – you already have the words you need to be a writer.

Things to beware of

THE THREE 'A'S; ADJECTIVES, ADVERBS AND ABSTRACT NOUNS

Thinking of a way *not* to begin a novel, the following comes to mind: 'It was a dark and stormy night. He walked slowly to the window and watched the devastation caused by the wind.'

Why do I object to this? (Apart from the opening sentence being famously bad.) The passage more or less sticks to Fowlers' recommendations: the language is everyday, it is concise – little wrong there. But how evocative are the words? How would it have been instead if I wrote: 'The moon was full. He shuffled to the window and watched the storm tearing at the limbs of the willow.' Any more of a picture?

Let's look at these two versions in detail: 'It was a dark and stormy night.' 'Dark' and 'stormy' are *adjectives*, words that describe a noun – 'night' in this case. Adjectives look as though they are doing something important, but are they? Exactly what did I mean by 'dark', and how stormy is 'stormy'? They are clues, to be sure, but they are inexact. A full moon, on the other hand, is exact: we know the quality of light, can picture it for ourselves. 'The storm tearing at the limbs of the willow' is likewise more in focus than 'stormy' alone.

Adjectives, in effect, are a shorthand. 'A beautiful young woman' for instance, really means 'You know what I mean. A beautiful young woman is the sort you see in magazines – all cheekbones and doleful eyes.' Multiplying adjectives in the hope of tightening the focus can mean we end up with a list: 'beautiful, almond-shaped, dark eyes' means almost nothing.

An *adverb* is a word which conditions a verb, telling us its quality. There is little justification for writing: 'He walked slowly.' English is a language bursting with verbs – use them. What exactly does the adverb 'slowly' mean? Edge, inch, creep, sidle, dawdle, slide, shuffle, wander, toddle? All these verbs evoke different pictures, and they are all, more or less, slow ways of walking.

Beware of unnecessary adjectives: '*happy* sound of laughter', '*gentle* caress' and unnecessary adverbs: 'she whispered *quietly*', 'he stared *fixedly*'. Superfluous adverbs weaken the narrative flow, for instance 'she went to him wordlessly' – if she doesn't say anything it is wordless. 'She went to him' is enough. This may seem picky, but anything that is superfluous is dead wood: every word must carry its weight.

Abstract nouns are naming words for states of mind or intellectual concepts or categories. An abstract noun, like an adjective or adverb, means different things to different people: what does 'happiness' mean? Or 'beauty'? 'Devastation', for instance, may mean a few flowerpots blown over, or it may mean an uprooted tree. The second version makes sure there is little misunderstanding: the wind is strong enough to tear at the limbs of the willow – no more, no less. Choosing an image rather than an abstract noun means there is less guesswork needed by your reader.

133

QUALIFIERS

Watch out for your use of qualifiers. A qualifier is a word which slightly alters the meaning of another, words such as 'quite', 'often', 'almost'. Qualifiers generally do nothing other than weaken your sentences – cut them out, unless by doing so the meaning of the sentence is significantly altered. What we sacrifice in accuracy, we gain in authority.

 ## William Strunk and E. B. White

'Rather, very, little, pretty – these are the leeches that infest the pond of prose, sucking the blood of words... we should all be very watchful of this rule, for it is a rather important one and we are pretty sure to violate it now and then.'

 ## Write

Write a passage in 300 words, using no adverbs, adjectives or abstract nouns, describing one of the following:

- A novice nun walking the length of a corridor, at the end of which is a thick studded door. Tall windows flood the corridor with light.
- A person on the flat roof of a tall city building, looking at the bustling city life below.
- An attendant in a Turkish bath soaping the back of a fat and hairy man.

When the piece is complete, add one adjective.

 ## Write

Take a passage from a novel by a writer whose style you admire. Analyse each sentence, looking for the author's use of verbs, nouns, adjectives, adverbs and qualifiers. What is the effect of their technical choices? Now write one of the scenes of the exercise above in the style of this author. Compare the effect of the original version with the second version.

IMAGERY: METAPHOR AND SIMILE

Abstract nouns are essentially 'telling', rather than 'showing'. Their use assumes readers know what the author intends because they have had a similar experience. But if you think your readers won't have experienced what you are talking about, or need help in imagining it, you can use an image: a metaphor or simile. For example, 'She was overcome by a feeling of complete *isolation*' (abstract noun), would mean different things to different people. 'She felt like a speck on the horizon' (simile), is more evocative, easier to grasp hold of.

Imagery needs to be handled with care: the author can be beguiled into thinking that an ingenious image is an effective one. Imagery may confuse a reader, or draw so much attention to itself that the reader is taken out of the story for a while. Either of these would work against your prime aim: to tell a story. 'Showing' with its no-nonsense literalness usually says more than even a well-chosen image: 'She heard the overpowering silence ringing in her ears', for instance, is probably the best of the three. Beware being poetic just for the sake of it.

Jean Cocteau

'A true poet does not bother to be poetical. Nor does a nursery gardener bother to scent his roses.'

CLICHÉS, SENTIMENTALITY AND RESPECTING THE READER

A cliché is defined by the Fowler brothers as 'a word or phrase whose felicity in a particular context when it was first employed has won it such popularity that it is apt to be used unsuitably or indiscriminately'. The first person who coined the phrase 'as cool as a cucumber' must have been delighted. The second person who said it had coined a cliché. A cliché is second-hand knowledge, betraying a lack of effort by the writer. A writer serving up clichés is in effect feeding his readers warmed-up left-overs.

Focus point

It's fine to use clichés in dialogue as long as you've decided that's how the character talks – don't let it happen accidentally.

At what point does sentiment topple over into sentimentality? When the writer is either so self-absorbed he or she has forgotten the reader exists, or when the writer stops respecting their discriminative faculties. Sentimentality is false emotion, failing to recognize, as it does, the complexity of a situation. It is also manipulative of the reader's emotions.

William Strunk and E. B. White

'No one can write decently who is distrustful of the reader's intelligence, or whose attitude is patronizing.'

Taking chances

Italo Calvino

'I am convinced that writing prose should not be any different from writing poetry. In both cases it is a question of looking for the unique expression, one that is concise, concentrated, and memorable. But digressions and loitering are also valuable.'

The more we think about style, the more self-conscious we can become, and we find our wings clipped. If we are too concise, too exact, too dutiful in our excision of superfluity, we can find ourselves editing the life out of our work. Digressions and loitering *are* valuable at times. It is worth keeping a certain craziness and irreverence in our writing. Marc Chagall, the Russian expressionist painter, said: 'I like to draw rather badly.' Letting the pen slip in your hand can have a beneficial effect – try it at times. Your job, remember, is to be an artist. There are no points for neatness.

Thomas Hardy

> *'The whole secret of a living style and the difference between it and a dead style, lies in not having too much style – being in fact a little careless, or rather seeming to be, here and there. It brings wonderful life into the writing.'*

Style is like a person, with all their shortcomings, flashes of brilliance, and vulnerability. A guarded, poised, elegant style may be admired in the way a person with those qualities might, but it will rarely be loved. Readers (with all their shortcomings, flashes of brilliance, vulnerability) want a friend, not a paragon.

Focus point

If you feel you are inhibited in your writing (perhaps your English teacher is always looking over your shoulder), then try writing something that you have decided to shred or burn as soon as it's finished. It could even be a letter to that English teacher explaining why you need your freedom.

Truly inspired writing takes chances. Unless you are willing to fail, you will never fully succeed. Grammar is not a cage within which the writer must live, but a convention formed by usage and improved upon by pedants. Split your infinitives if you like, use a preposition to end a sentence with. Good taste is something to be flouted. If you have a developed ear for language, the chances are you will get away with it.

There is only one way I know to marry spontaneity with discipline so that neither suffer: practise. Write again and again, editing your work with fair but firm hand, developing your craft so that your writing appears effortless. And then when people ask you the reason for your overnight success, you can reply: 'Ten years of practice.'

Workshop

Critically reading your own work is an important, difficult and risky task. Important because self-consciousness is a necessary part of creating a work of art: if we want to improve, we need to know our strengths and our weaknesses. Difficult, because critical distance from our own writing can never be truly achieved. And risky because self-consciousness is the enemy of spontaneity. These exercises are cautious moves in the direction of becoming self-critical readers. Transferring this rigour to the writing process can help you get it right first time.

- Take a piece of your own writing – perhaps a full chapter if you have one written – and strike out every adjective, adverb and modifier with a pencil. Now, taking a rubber, allow yourself only those words whose presence you can justify.
- Read a piece of your own writing over and over – both aloud and silently. Listen to the music of your sentences, ignoring the meaning. Notice any repetitiveness or cacophony. Mark sentences which appear clumsy, and then rewrite them, listening with your inner ear.
- Are there any words you overuse? Use a thesaurus to try to find some alternatives. Online 'word cloud' generators can help you identify your favoured words in a longer piece of writing.
- How would *you* describe your style? Look back over everything you have written. Do you think the style varies, or does it run through every piece? Try to sum up your style in a sentence.
- Now ask a friend or a member of your writing group to describe your style. Any surprises?

John Barth

'My feeling about technique in art is that it has about the same value as technique in love-making. That is to say, heartfelt ineptitude has its appeal as does heartless skill; but what you want is passionate virtuosity.'

Next step

In this chapter we've seen how style is a writer's journey of discovery. It's not about imitating a writer you admire, but about using language that comes naturally to you. While we have focused on cleaning up any unnecessary adjectives, adverbs and so on, we've also learned that it is important to take chances with our writing. In the next chapter we will be looking at how to use everything we've learned so far to develop and support the essence of your novel – its theme.

10

Theme

Theme is the heart of a story. Sometimes the theme will be clear before the first word is written, or sometimes the writer will start with a hunch and use the novel to discover exactly what to say. Either is fine; whether the theme is the impulse which gets you going or the point of arrival doesn't matter. What matters is that you have a theme, because without one, a story will never fully satisfy a reader, regardless of how well written it is, or how exciting, or how clever.

So, what is this important thing called 'theme'? The word is used to mean so many different things that I would like to drop its use for the duration of this chapter. In its place I suggest three levels of distinction:

- subject matter
- thread
- thesis.

Subject matter

The subject matter of the story is its tangible reality. The subject matter of *Jack and the Beanstalk*, for instance, is the consequences of selling a cow for five magic beans. If you hear someone say there are no original stories left to be told, they can't be referring to subject matter, for as the world is infinitely various, so is subject matter.

Genre fiction has a lot to say about subject matter, and if your novel falls into an obvious genre category, you should know what the current trends are. Having a good solid knowledge of similar genre novels is important, likewise knowing what others have said about such books. Trends, however, change quickly so you also need to keep your reading up to date. And not just of fiction: by the time a novel is in the bookshop it contains ideas at least two or three years old.

Focus point

Read newspapers, appropriate magazines, subscribe to a science-fction magazine, join the Romantic Novelists' Association, join Internet forums. Find out what other people are thinking and talking and writing about.

Try to spot trends – political, social, scientific. Michael Crichton had a particular knack of spotting a trend before anyone else.

If you want to raise your chances of making money, find a so-called 'high-profile' subject and give it an upbeat ending. You may not find a place in the twentieth-century hall of literary fame, but you may find an audience.

Write

Get hold of a copy of today's paper (you can look at most of them online, apart from *The Times*, which has a paywall). Choose a news story, a big one, and write a scene from the middle of the 'action'.

Steve de Souza

'The recipe for an Oscar winner: show a protagonist overcoming adversity against a background that exorcises the audience's guilt about an uncomfortable subject.'

Thread

A high-profile idea may get an editor's attention. Keeping it is another matter. This is where the thread plays its part. I use the word 'thread' for this level of distinction because, like a thread of cotton you might tie from tree to tree in an enchanted forest, it can help you retrace your steps if you get lost. A thread is a unifying idea, a line of thought that leads through a story upon which the plot events are strung like beads. There are a limited number of threads, the most obvious being:

- love
- survival
- guilt
- greed
- glory
- revenge
- justice
- redemption
- power
- freedom
- self-awareness
- vanity.

The thread of *Jack and the Beanstalk*? It depends how you tell it, but you could make a good case for 'greed'. Most novels contain a number of threads, in which case they should be plaited, that is, intricately combined.

Perhaps the best way to give an example of how threads combine is to tell you a complete story. This is one by the American writer Leonard Michaels.

The hand

I smacked my little boy. My anger was powerful. Like justice. Then I discovered no feeling in the hand. I said, 'Listen, I want to explain the complexities to you.' I spoke with seriousness and care, particularly of fathers. He asked when I finished, if I wanted him to forgive me. I said yes. He said no. Like trumps.

This is a classic plot – albeit rather brief. Although the story is not intended to stand alone (being a part of a collection of similar tales), it is a completed process of change, which upon close examination follows the eight-point arc. (Implied stasis; trigger is smacking the boy; quest to retain self-justification; the surprise is the hand going numb; critical choice to ask for forgiveness; climax, the son refuses to accept the apology; reversal, from dominant to dominated; implied resolution.)

The subject matter is always obvious: here, a father hitting his child and the conversation which follows. The threads of this tale are more a matter of personal interpretation: I think guilt and power are the threads in this case.

Focus point

You need to understand what the threads are in your story but you may find that readers see something quite different. This can come as a shock the first time it happens. All you can do is learn to live with it.

Snapshot

Choose three of your favourite books. Try to write down the 'threads' of each.

Thesis

The third level of distinction is that of thesis. This is the most important part of the three levels, the way to hold the editor's attention through the book and beyond. Whether readers can identify the thesis for themselves or not, it is what causes rumination after the book is finished, the element which generates debate and disagreement. And of the three levels, it is the most neglected by writers.

What is thesis? It can be defined simply as: *what the author is saying about the thread summed up in a single sentence.*

Snapshot

Stick with the three books you selected in the exercise above. Now try to write a single sentence that sums up the thesis of each story.

Angus Wilson

'The impulse to write a novel comes from a momentary unified vision of life.'

There is a story of how Winston Churchill once waved away a pudding in a restaurant after a single mouthful with the words: 'Take this pudding away. It has no theme.' A discriminating reader may say much the same thing about a novel with no thesis. A unified vision of life doesn't mean it has to be profound, but it can't be too confused. A pudding which is half Baked Alaska and half rhubarb crumble is confused. And anyway, most of us aren't seeking profundity from stories any more than we are seeking them from puddings. But we are seeking *comprehensibility*.

Let's look more closely at our definition of thesis:

What the author – in other words, you (not society, not received wisdom, not tradition)

is saying about the thread – what are you saying about greed? (What is Leonard Michaels saying about guilt and power?)

summed up in a single sentence – if the best you can come up with is a long and waffling explanation, it may be a sign your thesis needs attention. It may not be easy to do, you may have to think about it for months (I know I do), you may not know the thesis until you have reached the end of the book.

Key idea

Many books are extended debates between parts of the author. By the end the parts may agree to differ, or they may be integrated; either way they should reach a conclusion.

'A narrative is an argument stated in fictional terms.'

Don't let yourself off the hook with this. Being able to pin your thesis down – a kind of mission statement for the novel – will pay off. A clearly defined thesis can bring an entire novel into focus. A novel may be an argument, but it shouldn't be a stand-up row.

And a thesis, regardless of the complexity of the tale, can always be summed up in a single sentence (albeit a long one in some cases) without doing too much damage to its complexity. It was Einstein (I think) who said that anyone who couldn't explain his work to an eight-year-old is a charlatan.

It is perhaps *thesis* that people mean when they talk about there being a limited number of stories. But it is not the originality of your thesis, nor even its depth, which counts so much as the way you present it. Some perennial favourites include:

- Crime doesn't pay.
- You can't keep a good man down.
- Love conquers all.
- Hell hath no fury like a woman scorned.
- Winner takes all.
- The truth will out.

 ## Write

Choose one of the theses listed above and write a short story of no more than 1,000 words.

The thesis (and to some extent the thread) is not inherent in the bare bones of the story, its appearance figuring only in the telling. This is where the personality of the writer comes in: a single storyline can be presented in quite different lights without tampering too much with the eight-point arc. If any proof of this were needed, read about the same event in different newspapers. Without even distorting the facts, two very different views of a single event can be presented, depending on the prejudices and beliefs of the journalist.

Not only does the thesis depend on the telling, it depends on the interpretation by the reader. The meaning of a story, therefore, will always be open to debate – a fact for which critics are forever grateful, keeping them, as it does, in work. What is the meaning of the Leonard Michaels story? That guilt which turns to self-righteousness can be turned against the guilty? That the apparently powerless can still win the day? In a way, it is irrelevant if our understanding of the story differs from that of the author; what counts is that the author is clear in his own mind what he is doing. In this way, whether the story is completely successful or not, it will at least have a ring of authority.

Not every novel you read will have a clearly identifiable thesis: this may be because the author didn't manage to convey it in a way you could understand, or wasn't clear in the first place. Such books are often like low-grade fast food: tasty in an obvious sort of way, but without much nutrition. They can also leave you hungry, not because of a shortage of bulk, but because there's no substance behind the fizz and pop. The market for junk food and junk literature is ever expanding, and there is a lot of money to be made.

Focus point

Whatever sort of writing you are drawn to write, don't resist the tug. If you self-consciously inject meaning into your work, you will probably seem fake. Even junk has its own integrity.

The function of plot is to communicate the thesis. More than anything, stories fall down because of a lack of coherence. A series of events with little significance outside the drama of the story may just scrape by as a plot, but it will rarely outlive its creator.

Know your thesis

If the thread is a trail of cotton tied from tree to tree, the thesis is a compass keeping you pointing in the right way. If you have no compass, you won't know which way to go and could end up wandering for years. A wandering plot lacks shape because the directionless author doesn't know what fits in the story and what doesn't. Because, just as important as knowing what you *are* writing about is knowing what you are *not* writing about. A story which contains too many threads and not enough thesis is like a stew with too many ingredients – it ends up tasting of everything and nothing.

Plot events should be considered in the light of what you are saying about the thread: if 'crime doesn't pay' is your thesis (the thread could be greed), how would a scene between the criminal and his long-suffering partner contribute to that? It may legitimately contradict it: we may think for a while that crime *does* pay. Fine, as long as it is doing something there.

For every chapter, and every scene, you should ask yourself: what is it doing here? What does it say about the thesis?

Leo Tolstoy

'The most important thing in a work of art is that it should have a kind of focus, that is, there should be some place where all the rays meet or from which they issue.'

Snapshot

Think of the most recent novel you read, or film you saw. What were its threads? What was its thesis?

Snapshot

Analyse your work in progress. What are the threads? Do you have a thesis yet?

Hopefully, your structure will tell your readers what the thesis is without the need for explanation. You know you're on shaky ground when you have your characters doing a lot of talking at the end of the book; your readers may get the idea you're trying to explain your way out of a tight corner. Drama is about *action*, remember.

Key idea

A good plot is the manifestation of an idea in concrete, observable ways. You should be able to mime a good story and still convey the thesis.

The critical choices of your characters should be congruent with the thesis. If you can see no clear link between events precipitated by characters and what the story is saying, then you may find it is a weak link. If you sense a lull in activity in the middle of your book and throw in an exciting scene whose only function is to wake the reader up, then your reader may be confused. What was the meaning of the scene? Why did a man with a gun suddenly burst in and then leave for no apparent reason?

Such a scene may be one you have slaved over. You may be proud of its every word. It may contain the mostly finely honed sentences of your life. But if it doesn't contribute to the thesis, cut it out. Don't throw it away – you might be able to use it. Or if it's so good, shelve the novel and keep the scene. Whatever, don't be tempted to think that, just because it is your favourite scene, your readers will love it. If it doesn't contribute to the thesis, they'll wonder what it is doing there.

Edit

Take one of these deleted scenes and rewrite it as the first scene in a whole new novel.

Workshop

In this workshop we will reiterate some of the points made above in order to firmly establish the theme of your novel. Try to answer each of these questions as succinctly as possible and keep your answers to hand.

- What is your novel's subject matter? What genre are you writing in?
- What is the thread of your story, the unifying idea? Ask a friend to read your work – do they see the same threads running through the piece?
- What is the thesis? What is it that you are trying to *say*? Again, ask a friend or a fellow writer what they think your thesis is.
- What do you have to say about other things? As a writer, you should be up-to-date with current events and publishing trends. As you read the papers, note down what you think. You should be practising having opinions and expressing them well.

Go through your work scene by scene and make sure each adds to or supports your thesis. At the same time, ask yourself if any scenes exist solely to further the thesis. The action in your story should still follow a coherent plot structure. It's a story, not a think-piece.

Next step

In this chapter, we have learned that, while subject matter is the tangible reality of a story, the theme is its heart. We have looked at identifying and crystalizing the threads of a story and the thesis of your work as a whole, and how this can give your plot shape and coherence.

We have come a long way now, covering all the aspects of developing, shaping and writing your novel. In the next chapter, we will move on to look at what happens when you've actually finished your first draft.

11

The difficult business of second drafts

For me, all writing is rewriting. Absolutely no one has ever handed in a first draft and sat back to receive the rewards and the cheques.

When your book is accepted by an agent (and it will be), then he or she may very well work with you to reshape and rework it. They know the marketplace and they generally love good writing and know what sells, so you should listen to them (see Chapter 14). However, it is still your book. In the same way that a patient is usually the expert in their own complaint and needs to be able to stand up to the doctors, so the novelist is the expert in the narrow field of their own book.

At least some of the suggestions being made by your agent may have already occurred to you and been rejected. The agent may still be right, but you are under no obligation to them, save to listen courteously and to think seriously about their opinions. Respect their knowledge and experience, but have faith in your own judgement, too.

After an agent has helped you rework your project and sold it to a publisher, then your editor will want to go through the book, too. Editors have different requirements and styles: they might be quite hands on and want to substantially rework a novel you have already redrafted, or they might be more interested in marketing your book and not all that interested in the nuts and bolts of the text. They will definitely expect some changes, however, and that is before you've worked with a copy-editor and a proofreader, who really will want to go through your book with the finest of toothcombs.

Despite the fact that your book will go through several redrafts with agents and with editors, it is definitely best if you do as much of the editing as possible, before you send your manuscript out to anyone. Your book needs to be as polished as it can be before it goes out into the world. It only gets a first reading once and you want it to blow your reader away, and not have them trip up over an awkward plot, clunky paragraphs, unnecessary scenes and repetitions of favourite phrases.

Snapshot

Spend an hour or two online looking up your favourite writers' agents.

Writing and editing: don't get it right, get it written

If you've followed the practice as set out in this book, then you have broadly not tried to get your novel right; you have instead focused on getting it written. Your novel has been poured on to the page without too much in the way of stopping to reflect and with very little time spent on redrafting.

Like many supposedly iron rules, however, this one is made to be broken from time to time. Occasionally, I come back to work written in my last session and tidy and tinker and alter, before beginning the next section. I rarely attempt major structural alterations in a scene (though I will do from time to time).

For the most part, however, the important thing is just to get it down, to try to write steadily, regularly, with reasonable care, but trusting your instincts as an artist and listening to the internal critic on your shoulder as little as possible.

Composting

I'm a big believer that after the first draft you should wait. Allow the book to compost in a drawer while you catch up on the life you've missed. Your family and friends will be very glad to see you again. Go to the football, go to some parties, go on a romantic mini-break with your significant other, take your kids kayaking, see some bands, have some fun, and don't think about your novel. At all. This is an order.

Of course, you *will* be thinking about your novel; you're a novelist, you can't help yourself, but try to switch off as much as possible. Relegate your book to a place in your subconscious; let that dark and powerful figure have a go at your book with its shadowy editorial pencil.

This period should not be less than a month and probably not more than three months. Enough time to allow the white heat of creativity in which you finished the book to cool, but not so long that you lose touch with it.

And now you'll find a strange thing has happened: the changes that you need to make to your book become obvious. They come to light the way a message in invisible ink does under ultraviolet. So go through your book, reading slowly and making notes (now you see the need for having typed it double-spaced – it gives you adequate room to scrawl notes to yourself).

Don't attempt to read it on a screen. However wasteful it might seem, however environmentally unfriendly, you need to read from a hard copy. Read each scene aloud. You might feel fool foolish, but it's the easiest way to spot repetitions, inconsistencies in tenses and flawed phrases.

You will, I can assure you, reach a low point now. Your book, which seemed so good just a month ago, now looks like a condemned building. It feels like it needs to be torn down and rebuilt from the foundations up.

The chances are that, yes, you will have to revise everything, but if you've left enough time between drafts, new and better ideas will have occurred to you already. You'll have somehow – without even really thinking about it – accrued new material, much of it deserving of a place in the final text. And this is good because as well as areas that need expanding, there will be plenty from your first draft that need cutting.

Basically, now that you have begun your second draft you will need to be asking yourself whether the narrative devices you have chosen – probably instinctively – are the right ones. Tense, point of view, systems of images, metaphors and language – are they working?

 Key idea

> Cutting, reshaping and reworking may very well be the most creative stage of the whole writing process.

I promise you that once you begin editing your work, it will seem depressingly hard. Editing a novel is like climbing the same mountain, and on this second attempt you don't even have the thrill of conquering it to look forward to. Yet you've got to find a new route. And do it without crampons or spare oxygen. And there is actually no guarantee that you won't have to do it again – find yet another route, or do it blindfolded or naked.

So, yes, it will be depressing, but I can also promise that once you get properly into it, revising will create its own energy. You will find an excitement in it; you may even find yourself being intoxicated by the prospect of cutting. It'll be like having the best of all spring-cleans. 'That can go!' you may find yourself thinking. 'And that! And that! And that! And that! And what was I thinking when I wrote that? Into the delete file with you...!'

There will also be times when you smile at your work, and mentally give yourself a hug or a high five.

 Focus point

> It is important that you acknowledge the bits of your first draft that do work. Every now and then you will be amazed at something you've written. It is important that you savour these good moments. Reward yourself for them. (Even if it's just with a biscuit!)

DON'T KILL YOUR BABIES

One of the most quoted pieces of advice to new fiction writers is that of 'killing your darlings'. It was Arthur Quiller-Couch who said it first. What he actually said was this:

> Whenever you feel an impulse to perpetrate a piece of exceptionally fine writing, obey it – wholeheartedly – and then delete it before sending your manuscript to press. Murder your darlings.

Well, you sort of get what he means, don't you? Every word and every phrase has to fight for its place in your manuscript and anything that's flashy or self-consciously 'stylish' is almost certainly going to need to be cut. Everything you write should be rigorously tested and 'your darlings' probably more than most. Nevertheless, it seems odd to me that you should automatically get rid of anything that is most distinctively characteristic of your own voice and style.

Yes, we should be on high alert for anything that seems pretentious. And some of your work that seemed fine on a first reading may seem clunky when everything around it has changed. But generally I would argue that amid all the other cutting and change that goes on in a major edit, don't kill your babies – instead nurture them, work on them, improve them. Stylistic tics like these may be the very things that readers come to love about your work.

Edit

Go through your draft and identify your babies, those passages of writing you feel are particularly fine. Look them over with a stern eye and keep them under observation. Make sure they are as neat and well presented as possible – they will be your representatives in the world.

Points for revision

1 HAVE YOU BEGUN IN THE RIGHT PLACE?

A tendency many new writers have is to give everything away in the first chapter. Your first chapter's job is to grab the reader by the throat. To surprise them, to intrigue them, to make them feel they are in the safe hands of a master storyteller. A guide who will take them right to the edge of the precipice but who won't let them fall. Your first chapter should be like getting on the waltzer with a burly tattooed fairground hand behind you telling you to scream if you want to go faster.

Too often authors use the first chapter to fill in backstory and the CVs of their protagonists. That too should be drip-fed through the book.

Agents and editors often complain that a novel doesn't really get going until chapter three, in which case chapter three is really chapter one, isn't it?

2 IS THERE TOO MUCH BACKSTORY?

There will be information that you need to know about your characters but which your reader doesn't. You need to know their work history, their allergies, their romantic entanglements, but the reader needs only a fraction of that material. In a novel you are creating a dot-to-dot picture. You are the artist deciding where the dots go; it's for the reader to have the pleasure of joining those dots up and seeing the picture gradually appear.

Don't forget that the reader actually wants to write his or her own book. Every book is a collaboration between reader and writer. Every reader creates a different book from the reader that went before, and so you have to give them some room to put their own work in. Readers want to work; they don't want to be told everything. Your job is to give them the Lego kit, which will be theirs to build the police station or the airport or whatever they choose.

Less really is more!

3 ARE THERE UNINTENTIONAL REPETITIONS?

It would be surprising if there weren't. You've been writing at speed, concentrating on telling the story, and matters of style are the things that get overlooked, so this is the part where you read aloud to catch the repetitions and use a thesaurus to find inventive ways of expressing yourself. Or, rather, the right words. The words that are right for your characters, or for the voice of your novel.

4 IS ANYTHING IRRELEVANT?

I thought when writing it that my first novel, *TAG* (Cinnamon Press, 2008), might easily turn out be my last novel too, so into that book went every funny story I'd ever heard. Every good anecdote I had, every observation or thought I'd ever thought worth making. I told lots of stories in that book. Many of them good ones. And it was my agent who said: 'I like these stories, Steve. And you tell them well. But what on earth are they doing here?'

Yes, the reader wants a surprising mystery tour. Yes, they want surprises and deviations and twists. But they also want to feel the driver is safe, that he knows where he's going and can get them there in one piece. I was making my readers headachy and frustrated with the diversions I was taking them on. I was wearing their patience thin to the point of translucence. I lost nearly 80,000 words of irrelevant stories from my first draft, telling myself that each one might make a short story one day. And maybe one day they will, but they certainly had no place in that book.

> ## Write
>
> Look back over the bits and pieces you have cut from your work. Pick something you think could stand alone as a separate story and write a few paragraphs expanding this idea. If it fizzes, congratulations – you may have just found the beginning of your second novel. Now put it away and get back to editing your first one!

5 IS YOUR RESEARCH SHOWING?

I think it was the great novelist Fay Weldon who said 'Research is cowardice', by which I think she means that it is a way of avoiding writing your book. There is, after all, always more research you can do. Another friend of mine, an historical novelist of some repute, confessed to me that she does all her research from books meant for children: 'It's quicker, that way, and you don't get bogged down in detail.'

Historical novels can often seem flat because of the temptation to load the story up with interesting facts. The effect can be similar to the experience of sitting next to a boring uncle at a big family reunion, the one who knows everything about everything, except when to shut up. If you want your story to have good social skills, that is engage and intrigue readers, then you need to use research sparingly. Think of it as a powerful spice, like cloves or nutmeg, and be careful with it for fear of ruining the dinner that has, after all, taken a very long time to prepare.

6 IS THERE ANY DEAD WOOD?

The answer is yes, almost certainly. For a start, every sentence over 30 words is almost certainly too long. You have almost certainly repeated the same thought or idea several times in an attempt to make sure that the reader REALLY GETS IT. There is no need for this. Readers are smart, and not only that: they want to work hard and to puzzle things out and make their own connections.

You probably have characters, too, who don't really earn their keep. Readers don't like characters who come in, do one thing and disappear. The entrance of Helmut the plumber raises all sorts of expectations in the reader. Is he the killer? A potential love interest? A spy? So when Helmut simply fixes the boiler and disappears for ever from the story, readers feel cheated. Helmut is, on this occasion, the deadest of wood.

Similarly, does the stasis from which each scene begins last too long? And equally, and just as irritatingly for readers, is your resolution too long? There is a sense in which *all* books are thrillers. Yes, even *Howards End* and *The Great Gatsby*, even your carefully crafted comedy of manners set in the court of Emperor Ferdinand II of Spain. Every book is wide-screen entertainment, just of – hopefully – a complex and sophisticated kind.

 Focus point

All books need to be page-turners at some level. When in doubt – cut. And then cut some more. You'll get to like it, trust me.

There is, of course, also the danger that we can edit all the charm and uniqueness out of our book. As Pliny the Younger put it: 'Too much polishing weakens rather than improves a work.'

Editing sentences and paragraphs is a matter of getting a feel for the music of the language. Check the text is coherent – pay attention to aspects such as tenses and viewpoint. Ensure that it works as a piece of language, that there is some poetry in there, that it sings. Brevity counts for a lot. Be bold. Aim for a slim book if you can.

Shaping the novel

It is actually only when you finish the novel that you can finally know the extent of its theme. That is, what it's really about. And it's only in reading it through carefully again, that you can catch the defining tone of the piece, so a lot of editing means working steadily through making sure this is seamless and that it feels of a piece. Symphonic, if you will.

Your story needs to have a clear beginning, middle and end. So much is obvious. But it also needs tension to mount throughout the book. At the same time it shouldn't appear to move too fast or the reader will feel battered and bruised by the end, like they've been in a hurricane.

Remember the eight-point arc introduced earlier (Chapter 3)? We can see that this means: beginning = stasis, trigger and quest; middle = surprises, critical choices and climax; end = reversal and resolution. But scenes themselves also need the same kind of dramatic structure, so the major arc of the story will contain minor arcs within its scenes and its chapters.

As well as drama, you need to ensure you build in *andante* passages – quieter periods, lulls where the reader gets to pause, take a breath and enjoy the view.

Another thing you might want to try is to draw the shape of your novel. Or map it as though it was a journey through a wilderness. Or imagine that you a designing a roller-coaster. Of course, if you've had the guide of a good but flexible synopsis, you won't have got entirely lost through the journey of your novel, but it will be amazing how many deviations and digressions from the path there are anyway. And of course some of these may be necessary, enjoyably frustrating cul-de-sacs for the reader.

The art of good style

The real point of getting rid of all the clutter is to highlight your style, to allow it to shine. If you write in your own way, and do it regularly, you will, eventually, find your voice. You'll find a style which is unique to you and which you feel comfortable with. Cutting will be part of the process of clearing away all that is superfluous, anything that doesn't fit your style or your strategy.

STUDY EXCELLENCE

A lot of novelists claim not to read fiction while they write in case it influences them. I would say instead that influence is what you hope for. It would be extraordinary for a musician or songwriter to claim they listened to no music while recording an album, or for a painter to avoid art for the duration of a painting.

One of the great things about being an artist in the modern era is that everything is available for you to study. Everything, from all of recorded history more or less. Every book, from the *Epic of Gilgamesh* to a marginal novel self-published online yesterday: all of it is there for you to study and learn from.

As long as you read widely enough and are disciplined and focused enough to keep your own novel at the forefront of your mind, then other writers' voices, strategies and solutions to problems will inform your own. One thing is certain. Even if your novel doesn't get published (and it will), then writing a book will make you a better, more careful, more appreciative reader.

Unlike aspiring Olympians, emerging writers can be mentored by the very best talents from the history of literature, and get their input at the moment when they are at the top of their game. Imagine being a footballer with talent: you are unlikely to get Beckham or Messi to teach you the finer aspects of the game. But for writers, the likes of F. Scott Fitzgerald, E. L. Doctorow, Martin Amis, J. D. Salinger, Sarah Hall, Suzanne Berne, Sarah Waters, Fay Weldon, John Irving, Daniel Defoe and Laurence Sterne are all waiting just to teach you everything they know.

It's as Stephen Fry said: 'An original idea? That can't be hard. The libraries must be full of them.'

Snapshot

I hope this one doesn't feel too much like homework! Write a list, now, of ten books you have always meant to read but have never got round to. Make a commitment to yourself to finish them all in a year. Read in the bath, on your commute, before you go to bed at night. If you feel like you don't have time, give up a TV show or two. Treat reading like an athlete treats their training – as vital.

THE ENEMIES OF GOOD STYLE

Cliché

A cliché is a phrase that has become stale with overuse and in a novel this can also include stock situations, visual images and so on. One problem with being a novelist, working away on your own, is that you may not actually know what has become a cliché.

Reading a wide variety of contemporary novels will help, but still you won't necessarily be aware that of the million manuscripts in agents' offices in London and New York, 250,000 begin with their single thirty-something protagonists waking up with a hangover. You won't know that another 250,000 include lyrical descriptions of the dust motes as they dance in the rays of the late-evening sun that beams in through the windows.

Then again, my second novel begins with a description of a funeral and I was later told by a respected creative writing professor that she always advised her students against doing such a thing. And the thing that's really funny about that is it was my publisher who told me to do it. Once again, it's sensible to keep in mind that rules can always be broken.

Key idea

Good style has a lot to do with freshness of vision.

Snapshot

Take one of the scenarios listed above – the dust motes, the hangover or the funeral – and try to write a paragraph or two that flips the clichés on their heads.

Sentimentality

Carl Jung said: 'Sentimentality is a superstructure covering brutality.' In a novel, sentimentality is usually caused by over-writing a scene featuring a character that you care for. It's very easily done when that character is facing a moment of extreme crisis. It is essential to read these passages with the flintiest of hearts, and be particularly receptive to criticism your trusted gang of early readers may have about these passages. Another reliable guide is that, if you feel a scene might be too sentimental, then it probably is.

A lack of heart

This is the opposite problem from the danger of sentimentality. In your efforts to produce a compelling, page-turning novel you might have forgotten to allow readers to fall in love with your characters. Remember to give opportunities for your characters to reveal their positive qualities in action.

Clumsy phrases

These are phrases which jar and which will break the spell you are trying to enchant the reader with. An awkward, anachronistic or out-of-character phrase is sometimes all it takes for a reader to put down the book with a sigh and start thinking about unloading the dishwasher. Reading aloud is the best way of identifying these nasty little booby-traps.

Too many adjectives and adverbs

This is a common mistake for first-time novelists. Happily it's an easy fix. Adverbs tend to be the mark of lazy writing, or of writing that was rushed. They tell us what someone thinks or feels rather than show us. If someone 'crawls wearily' or 'snaps angrily', then the adverb is implied by the action and is consequently redundant. Make sure every adverb really fights for its place in your fiction.

Adjectives have a dulling effect on a piece of prose, limiting the reader's own imagination and suggesting that the writer lacks confidence. It implies that they can't quite manage to describe a person or event properly and are straining for effect. It makes readers worry that they are not in safe hands. That maybe the pilot isn't sure how to land the plane.

Snapshot

Go through your novel and highlight all the adverbs and adjectives. One by one, ask yourself, 'Is this really necessary?' Be ruthless.

Poor punctuation

Contrary to popular opinion, publishers still expect writers to be able to sort out their own punctuation and spelling. If your manuscript is so error-strewn as to suggest the writer is borderline illiterate, it won't even make the slush-pile. It will go in the bin.

If you can, ask a teacher friend to read your manuscript through for you, red pencil at the ready. Do this even if you're a teacher yourself or otherwise very proud of your grammar. Everybody slips up sometimes and it can be hard to spot your own mistakes.

Novel length

A novel should be exactly 256 pages.

This is a joke (obviously, I hope). A novel can't be any fixed length; it is as long as it needs to be. When writing your first draft you should just be thinking of what happens next, of making sure you progress through your chosen arc or mythic journey.

However, in a second draft maybe you need to think about this more seriously. Anything under 60,000 words is probably too short for a first-time novelist hoping to get published by a mainstream publisher. And 40,000 words or less isn't really a novel, it's a novella. It'll make publishers nervous because readers like to relax into a book and something so short may not allow them to do that. Also, readers may be wary of forking out full-price on what looks like half a book. It'll be interesting to see if the popularity of ebooks changes things at all, but for now if you want to publish a very short book you might have to wait to become famous first. One successful writer I know found that her contracts began to include a clause that her novels would be at least 90,000 words long.

Equally, a very long book can be off-putting for some readers, though genre seems to play a part here. Readers of historical epics or fantasy books seem to like their books upwards of 200,000 words long; they like the sprawl through time and to feel they are in for a long ride. Readers of literary fiction seem to value concision rather more. As a general guide, ideally aim for 70–100,000 words for a first novel, but keep in mind, really how long is that piece of string?

CHAPTER LENGTH

The same goes for chapters, they should be as long as they need to be and go through their own story arc. I would say as a general rule that they should perhaps be no longer than the amount the average reader can consume in a single reading session.

They should also be consistent. A very short chapter followed by a very long one can be jarring for a reader and make them feel unsettled. There are exceptions, of course. You may have a minor character far away from the main body of the action whose life we need to check in on every now and again, and those chapters might be shorter. As a general rule though we should try to have some empathy with the reader and the balance they always have to strike between losing themselves in a book and getting the kids' tea, or otherwise getting on with life.

Finishing your book

When can you truly say that your book is finished? Well, in one sense you can't. It was Guillaume Apollinaire who said about poems that they 'weren't ever finished, they were abandoned'. I think the same holds true for any work of art. You stop working on it because you have an absolute, unshakeable, immovable deadline, or because you're making the book worse rather than better. Or because the new project – the next novel – is beginning to push its way forward, demanding to be written.

In the first draft of your book, you are really telling the story to yourself. It can be quite freeform – even if you are a writer who likes to stick to a plan – like jazz. The next draft is to make sure that there is a coherent structure written in your unadorned, unaffected voice. It's also the time for cutting unnecessary sections and expanding those that seem undeveloped. It's the time for killing adverbs and hunting down clichés and clumsy phrases.

Further drafts bring you closer to your goal, deepening the depth of focus and giving the book more heart, more soul. Making it more the book it should be.

To do this effectively, it is a good idea to bring in your trusted readers after a second or third draft – when it's polished, but not yet finished. And really listen to what they have to say. It might also be the time to go on a course, or to submit your work to an editorial consultant, or find some other form of support. No one can do it all on their own.

Key idea

Good enough, sometimes, really is good enough. Know when to let go.

Write

Write a review of your second draft as though you were not the writer. Note the things that work and those that don't.

Workshop

Ask yourself the questions listed above. Have you begun in the right place? Is there too much backstory? Are there any unintentional repetitions? Is anything irrelevant? Is your research showing? Is there any dead wood?

As you work through your draft, highlight or underline any passage that you particularly like – your 'darlings'. Be extra careful when editing these. Are there any superfluous adjectives, adverbs, qualifiers and so on? Can you sense any tinge of purple? You don't have to kill your darlings, but you do have to make sure they look their best.

Ask yourself how well your story fits within the eight-point plot arc. Can you match each point with a scene or event from your novel?

Remember to spellcheck the living daylights out of your manuscript. Read it aloud and get other people to read it. If you want to be really thorough, read it backwards – it's a great way to spot spelling errors or typos you may have previously missed.

Finally, ask yourself these questions. What are my novel's successes? Which parts am I most pleased with? What are my strengths as a writer? Remember, finishing a draft of a novel is a huge achievement and, while there is a lot of work ahead, you should take the time to congratulate yourself for how far you've come.

Next step

In this chapter we have learned that editing is of paramount importance. While writing is inspirational, editing is a craft. You need to have high standards in your spelling, punctuation and grammar. You need to be a bit ruthless. But you also need to give yourself credit for completing the very difficult task of writing a novel. Because I know just how hard it is, the next chapter contains some tricks and tactics to get you through the dark times when 'writer's block' rears its head.

12

Writer's block

The road to writing a novel is – as both The Hollies and Sir Paul McCartney have pointed out – long, with many a winding turn. And it is inevitable that you'll run out of fuel at various points. Hopefully this is temporary, you just need a breather. Take in the view. Think about something else for a while. Sometimes the condition doesn't just clear up on its own. When that happens, you have writer's block. Don't panic; everybody gets it, and nearly everyone works their way out of it too.

Technical and non-technical writer's block

When Nigel Watts wrote the first edition of this book, he identified two types of writer's block: technical and non-technical. He asserted that of these, technical writer's block was the easiest to deal with, by methods such as doing more research so that you can maintain credibility in the story, or deepening your understanding of your characters so that they come alive, or plotting more thoroughly so that you can proceed with the story telling.

Non-technical writer's block is the result of something other than the story. And if this is the case, then you won't find the answers on the page. They are, however, quite often found by going for a walk. I'm a big fan of walking. I think walking pace is the proper speed of thought. We are hunter-gatherers, meant to run in short bursts infrequently and to spend the rest of the time sleeping, walking, eating handfuls of berries and telling stories. Walking and writing are the same thing in many ways. Walking along, muttering to ourselves, is certainly one of the quickest ways to unblock a story. Fresh air, a raise in the pulse, the sensation of steadily moving forward, taking time to notice both the amazing view and the tiny flowers by the road. And making a mental note of odd incongruous sights – the rusting Morris Oxford in a field, the high-fashion shoe in a stream – all of these are proper writerly activities and analogous to putting together a story that grips.

 ## Hilary Mantel

'If you get stuck, get away from your desk. Take a walk, take a bath, go to sleep, make a pie, draw, listen to music, meditate, exercise; whatever you do, don't just stick there scowling at the problem. But don't make telephone calls or go to a party; if you do, other people's words will pour in where your lost words should be. Open a gap for them, create a space. Be patient.'

Focus point

Going for a walk is another form of writing – walking speed is the proper pace of thought. All things become clear on a walk.

Snapshot

Put this book down and go for a walk. It doesn't need to be a long one, half an hour or so is fine. Keep your eyes open. When you get back, make a list of at least ten things you saw. One of them might be the seed of a new story.

Sometimes I think our story needs to be moved to the back-burner and left alone for a while. Just as a watched pot never boils, sometimes a story needs time to simmer on its own.

Focus point

Sometimes being a writer means leaving your desk and doing something else for a while. Walking, swimming, digging the garden, chopping wood – something where you are alone with your thoughts.

Physical blocks

Sometimes our physical environment is at odds with our ability to produce our best work. It might be that you need a new chair or a decent desk. You might need a computer that doesn't make strange buzzing noises. You might need to start writing in the library, or at a different time of day. Sometimes a simple change of scene will do the trick.

Edit

Assess your writing environment. What does it say about the importance of writing in your life? What do you want it to say? What changes do you want to make? Edit your space so there is nothing unnecessary there, no extraneous items or distractions.

Exercise might unblock you. Writers lead notoriously unhealthy lives, so taking up a sport might counteract lethargy or fatigue. Alcohol, caffeine, cigarettes and complicated love lives are also not friends to writers, despite what Ernest Hemingway tried to get us all to believe. It is sad but true that for most of us the best conditions for writing are those recommended by the Scout movement: fresh air, exercise, a good night's sleep, a healthy diet. In order to write well we should try to live like a well looked-after Labrador.

Gustave Flaubert

'Be a bourgeois in your life so you can be an anarchist in your art.'

Sound advice if you are writing a novel.

Emotional blocks

Hemingway (I know, him again) said you should 'write hard about what hurts', but it's hard to do this. Sometimes we lock in feelings that demand an outlet and the pressurized contest between the desire to go somewhere dark and the fear of what we might find there causes a kind of stasis. We know we have to pick over memories that are hard to process, but it doesn't make it any easier to do. Or we might need to write something that we think others will find difficult to hear. But your truth is valid and, although you shouldn't be wantonly destructive, you might only be able to move on in your novel when you acknowledge your right to tell your version of the truth in the way you can.

Psychological blocks

Psychological blocks are the result of negative beliefs of long standing. I began writing seriously in 1998, a year that was dominated by two major life events: (1) My father dying and (2) meeting my wife.

My father was a clever bloke. An autodidact, he had grown up in quite extraordinary poverty with undemonstrative parents. His father died when he was in his teens and my dad worked hard to get himself an education that would mean he could escape the soul-grinding desperation of the life many others of his class had to endure. There was no prospect of university. He was, deep down, kind-hearted but he was also thwarted and difficult, competitive with his children. A man who always had to be right, who was capable of incredible, bewildering rages that came at unpredictable times. He also drank way too much. I loved him, of course I did, but I was afraid of him for a long time – and also afraid that I would grow to be like him.

My dad wanted his children to be clever and do well. But he didn't actually want them to be cleverer or do better than he had, so he was quite belittling of any effort to develop, particularly if it was at something creative. Partly this was a simple fear of destitution. In my dad's world artists tended to starve or needed someone else to support them, and he didn't want it to be him.

My first short play with a professional cast was produced just a couple of months before he died and when I rang – naturally excited – to tell him, he said, 'Well, don't expect me to come. I hate the New Theatre.' And I was quite upset. And puzzled. What was this thing called the New Theatre, and why did he think I was going to be writing it?

Even now I'm a bit shocked. Can you imagine saying that to a child – even a grown-up one – that you wouldn't come and see their work? And for that to be your first reaction? Still, he was as good as his word because he didn't see it. He couldn't. He died suddenly a few weeks later. I was devastated by his death. But it's also become clear to me that my dad's personality and domineering presence had acted as a break on all my efforts at self-expression (he wasn't the only retarding influence – I also laid plenty of traps for myself without his help).

I tell this story, because it might be that you have similar roadblocks stopping you telling your stories. You can't wait around for the obstacle to remove itself. You need to identify it, confront it and move on from it.

 Focus point

Negative feelings are like cockroaches. They don't like the light. Shine a torch into the murky crevices where they hide and you might find they disappear quicker than you ever thought possible.

One thing is certain: ignoring your negative feelings about yourself will hold you up. People worry that they are not academic enough to be a good writer; or not imaginative enough; or that they'll be attacked for saying what they think or feel. People often feel that writing books is 'not for the likes of them' and this is often because at some unconscious level a teacher, or a parent, has told them this. Or somehow they have imbibed it from the mass media, where, it is true, most writers seem to come from the Oxbridge-attending classes. But you don't need to be academic to write books. You don't need an off-the-wall imagination and everybody has the right to express themselves.

Some unblocking techniques

If it does turn out to be something a walk in the park can't fix (the
literary equivalent of turning a computer off and then on again),
then here are some techniques which might help (again, I'm indebted
to Nigel Watts here for some – but not all – of these solutions):

FREE WRITING

The idea is to shake the critic from your shoulder and to let your
subconscious – that extra gear we all have – take on some of the
responsibility for the propulsion of your story. What you write might
be entirely rubbish – but I bet it isn't. I bet there are some diamonds
in the dung heap there. I bet there are ideas or fragmentary phrases
that you can work with.

Refinements of this technique might include writing a list of words that seem to sum up the scene you are working on. Keep these simple, for example, 'Light' or 'Dark' or 'The Beach'. Repeat the exercise as before, but this time if you feel yourself slowing down glance at your list and use one of your target words to propel you forwards again. The important thing is not to stop, no pausing even for a second.

Another way to resolve an apparently intractable impasse is to take whatever is in your pockets and to use that as a stimulus. What you're attempting to do is to inject some surprise into your work, a sense of the random, to circumvent the rational brain and whatever is holding it ransom. To find a new, perhaps more scenic, route home.

CHANGE THE TOOLS

Try writing your next scene with a pen in longhand, or even (gasp!) use a typewriter. Your hand, wrist and eyes will all hurt, you'll be frustrated at the mistakes you make, but this is all part of cudgelling your brain out of the rut it is plainly stuck in.

Also, sometimes PCs make writing too easy, too much of a downhill race. Sometimes what you need is resistance. There are practical advantages to this too. The physical contact with the words makes writing much more of a craft, on a par with painting or with thatching a roof. With my first novel, *TAG*, I wrote nearly all of it on a laptop, but there were times when I found myself stranded without it, and those few parts written by hand were hardly redrafted at all. Everything else was changed around a lot, but those bits could be pretty much left alone. Coincidence? Maybe, but probably not.

You could also try one of Nigel Watt's old tricks – he used to have a dialogue in writing about why he was stuck. His non-dominant hand would take the voice of his positive self saying the things he could feel good about, while his dominant hand got to express any negativity about his life as a writer. He would write, passing the pen back and forth between hands, until he reached a natural end. He was, of course, always careful to make sure that the positive hand got the final say!

USE A SABOTAGE PAGE

As you write, have another piece of paper with you and any time a negative thought comes along to prevent your flow, write it down. There's no need to deal with it. You've acknowledged it and sometimes that's enough. Once written down negative thoughts are revealed in all their ridiculousness and disappear.

END THE WRITING SESSION IN THE MIDDLE OF A SCENE

Or even in the middle of a line. That way when you come to sit down at the beginning of the next session you should just be able to pile in. Having your start ready-made might make it easier to fire up the whole system. Not unlike jump-starting a car in fact.

GIVE YOURSELF A BREAK

Don't do this too often, but we've all had the experience where we've been driving ourselves mad looking for something (TV remote, specs, keys, book) and only find it when we put it out of mind, convincing ourselves that it has gone for ever. Sometimes just walk away whistling for a while, and when you come back the solution to the knotty passage may be obvious.

Writing as an organic process

Sometimes your idea just isn't ready to germinate yet. Writing a book is not like making a model or mass producing widgets of any kind. It's much more like landscape gardening. Or like working in a glass house with some temperamental orchids. Things grow in their own time and in forcing the pace you can kill the thing entirely.

Workshop

At the start of each day, assess all your commitments and ask yourself where you can slot in a writing session – however short. Could you skip a soap opera? Get up a bit earlier? Go to bed later? Cull a few friends? Find some time and then stick to it, whatever happens.

Reward yourself for reaching deadlines. Carrots are better than sticks. Give yourself a small reward for reaching an ordinary milestone (end of a page, end of a scene, writing 500 good words) and bigger rewards for bigger milestones (every 10,000 words, say).

If you find yourself getting stuck a lot, ask yourself if something bigger is at work. Are you psychologically blocked? Do you feel, perhaps subconsciously, that you are not good enough to be a writer? Not clever enough, or wordy enough, or committed enough? Sit down and pour it all out on to paper. Force your demons into the blistering sunlight. Maybe even write a short story in which those little gremlins are personified and then vanquished.

If you find yourself getting down, try something completely different. Write something silly, just for fun. Try one of these writing prompts – no pressure!

- Write a limerick about your least favourite high-school teacher.
- Write a short story in which animals reveal they have been able to talk all along.
- Turn on the TV and write a monologue from the point of view of the first person you see.
- Remind yourself why you want to write a novel.

Next step

In this chapter we've seen that everyone gets blocked sometimes, and that giving in to negative feelings about your ability as a writer will only delay your novel. I've shared a few tips and techniques that will hopefully spur you on again, but remember not to beat yourself up – it's just a book! In the next chapter though, we'll look at places where you can find some support on your journey to being a novelist and perhaps meet some like-minded people.

13

Support

No one does anything entirely on their own. And that's as true of novels as it is of anything else. Remember the 2012 London Olympics? Every single one of those gold medal winners had a whole team behind them. Even Usain Bolt, even Mo Farah, even those amazing American women who blew the field apart in the 4 × 400 metres relay. Yes, they've put the work in. Yes, it's the athletes who turn up in all weathers, however they're feeling, and put the hours and the miles in, but there are also coaches and physios and doctors working behind the scenes, not to mention all those people closer to home: the husbands and wives and friends and fellow athletes.

Of course, writing a novel is a marathon, not a sprint. In fact, it's an ultra-endurance marathon across the least hospitable terrain known. And for most of us there are no sponsors, and the training is the whole game. If there is any applause from spectators, it comes after the event is over, when we're in the middle of our next project. This makes a support network all the more important. Fortunately, as a writer beginning your novel at this point in the twenty-first century, there is more readily available support than there has ever been.

There are, of course, more distractions and more pressures than there have ever been too. But as well as gathering allies and support, there are things we can do for ourselves. You've reached Chapter 13 of this book, so we've established that you're serious about this project and now you owe it to yourself to consider what help you can find to make sure you complete the course, and are in the best position to compete for any medals going.

The physical environment

Most people know Virginia Woolf's declaration, that every writer needs a room of their own. I know one successful writer who has a flat of his own, a two-bed place he only uses for writing. Not that I'm jealous (much). I am lucky enough to have a spare bedroom at home I can use. And the most useful thing in that room is the door. I can close it. And I can put a notice on it warning (begging) people to keep out. If people come knocking on that door when I'm in there, they know they had better have a very good reason. Wanting to show me the lovely picture they've drawn of a flower or a battlefield is not good enough. It sounds harsh, but we owe it to our book to create the right environment, both for us and it.

I don't think you need to be in a particularly inspirational space to write. It doesn't need to have a literary history, or have magnificent views. Franz Kafka had the idea of a burrow, a place where there was so little external stimulation that the imagination was forced to create, to intervene and create a landscape and characters. Writing a novel is a kind of prolonged madness, complete with voices in the head and other vivid hallucinations, and the more you can to do to aid, and then channel, this process the better.

So no expensive desk, no view over Lake Windermere, not even a shed in a garden. You just need a place that becomes sacred to the act of writing while you're doing it. And you need to let everyone else know this. So tell them. The more people who know that you identify yourself as a writer the better. And it is also important that they know, not just that you are a writer, but that you are one with a big project.

Respect your writing space too. Whether it is a writing flat like the one my friend has, a spare room like mine, or just a desk in your bedroom, make sure that it only has the material connected to your novel in it. Only stuff that will help your work. So no unpaid bills or postcards, or catalogues from clothing companies.

Key idea

Recognizing the importance of writing for yourself and declaring it to other people will help establish it in your life. Make sure this is reflected in the way you model your writing space. When it's yours, everything about it should say 'Caution: Writer at Work'.

Snapshot

Commandeer your space and make it yours. Find something to make it feel special, like a beautiful mug to hold your pens or a framed picture you find inspiring.

Stephen King

'People think that I must be a very strange person. This is not correct. I have the heart of a small boy. It is in a glass jar on my desk.'

Time

Everyone has time to write. Yes, even you. But free time won't come knocking at your door; you will have to make the space for it. It's true that you might have some adjustments in your life. You might have to get up an hour earlier. You might have to stop watching movies or the TV. Crucially you might have to stop surfing the Internet quite so much. Yes, you can call it research all you like, but it looks incredibly like procrastination from where I'm sitting.

It used to be said that success in writing was 1 per cent inspiration and 99 per cent perspiration. And I'm inclined to think it's now at least 50 per cent about not being distracted by the blandishments of the web. I have enormous concentration problems and so I got rid of my television in order to write, but with wireless Internet, television is always with you. In fact, the whole noisy multimedia jibber-jabber of the world is only a click away. It takes enormous discipline and focus to get anything done.

Snapshot

If you struggle with the temptations of the Internet, consider investing in a programme like Freedom. This allows you to set a timer for anything up to eight hours, during which time your computer is disconnected from the web. This allows you to write for a set time without being interrupted by videos of cute cats or quizzes to ascertain which Disney villain you are most like.

Ray Bradbury 'The Internet is a big distraction. It's distracting, it's meaningless; it's not real. It's in the air somewhere.'

WORK IS A FOUR-LETTER WORD

Many of us have day jobs, and that's OK. Many writers have had to hold down jobs. Famously there was T. S. Eliot in a bank, Kafka in an insurance company, Larkin at Hull University library, all of them producing honed and crafted work while in senior management positions. Admittedly, that was before jobs demanded all of our lives. Laptops and smartphones have meant that the office comes to us at all times of the day or night, and it can be a hard mistress to ignore.

But ignore it you must. Even if it's just for a short while every day. Just like you must ignore your family and your friends.

WRITING EVERY DAY

And, if you can, try to make sure you ignore all the distractions and write every single day. The great American novelist Suzanne Berne – winner of the Orange Prize – told me that with a busy family and a job she despaired of finishing her first book. In the end she made a pact with herself, she would find five minutes every day. If she managed it, she would put a tick on the calendar that hung in her kitchen. She became obsessed with getting her daily tick. In fact, writing the book became almost secondary to getting the all-important tick. The beauty of this sort of system is, that if you tell yourself that, hey, it's only five minutes, then quite often you'll find that you've managed 15 minutes or 20 and substantial novels can be written in a year in this way.

I suppose the point I'm making is that you need much shorter chunks of time in which to work than you perhaps think. Yes, five minutes is probably too short for most people, but half an hour is enough time to get some concentrated work done. To make some progress. And an hour can feel like a luxury sometimes.

But it's the regularity that is the key. Getting into a habit. It should become so that you feel very grumpy if you don't manage to get some writing done. And this grumpiness should be so painfully irritating to those around you, that they become coaches as well as cheerleaders, making you sit at your table and write even when you don't want to. Sometimes it's a case of replacing bad habits with better ones that are just as addictive.

Focus point

Even ten minutes each day is long enough to write and make progress.

DAYDREAMING IS THE JOB TOO

One thing to be wary of is that to the untutored eye a lot of writing simply looks like daydreaming. It looks like it, because that is what it is. Staring at the wall, writing a note down, then a few moments later crossing that note out again. All of this is work and needs to be defended too. The staring at the wall time is important; you'll write nothing good without it.

IF YOU CAN'T WRITE, DO NOTHING ELSE

I think it was Raymond Chandler who said that he had a set writing period of two hours. Sometimes he lacked inspiration and he couldn't make the words flow. Chandler decided to be relaxed about this. If he didn't write anything in those two hours, well, so be it. The key to his method, however, was that he didn't allow himself to do anything else in his writing time. If he couldn't continue with his story, he wasn't allowed to go for a walk, wash the car or make dinner. He just had to sit and look at the typewriter. He didn't have to write, but he was forbidden from doing anything else. Quite often, sheer boredom forced him to bust through the mental chains.

Again, with the Internet singing its siren songs, tempting you with its many amusing videos of cats doing the funniest things, then just sitting and staring at the laptop without 'just' checking your emails, or Facebook, or Twitter demands proper discipline.

TREAT EMAILS AS IF THEY WERE THE POST

By which I mean only check your mailbox once a day. Another writer friend of mine has a rule that he doesn't check emails until 4 p.m. His theory being that still gives you enough time to answer anything really urgent within the normal working day, but stops you being sucked into that nightmare email vortex where you are copied in on something which you comment on, which is then copied to someone else, who comments, prompting you to reply, and so on. Hours are lost this way. Days. Weeks. Months. Years. Whole novels stolen by a routine enquiry or piece of banter that wasn't really for you in the first place.

Sensible advice that I hope one day to be grown up enough to follow myself.

TOO MUCH TIME

It is definitely possible to give yourself too much time. A new writer I know was lucky enough to find that he could give up work for a year. Finally, he could devote himself to his writing. He was determined not to waste this precious year. He was, quite sensibly, going to treat writing with the same respect and dedication he'd brought to other jobs he'd had. And this particular friend of mine is a conscientious man. So every morning, he took himself off to his writing room at nine and laboured steadily at his novel until 5 p.m. Quite often he would edit and revise in the evenings too. After six months he'd finished. After nine months he'd redrafted it and felt it was ready to show to agents. They quite liked it. He got a lot of nice notes back and some good feedback. But no one loved it. No one wanted to take it on. The feedback was that somehow it lacked that vital spark. It didn't have it – that ineffable thing that raises a piece of writing out of the commonplace, that gets it off the slush pile and between hard covers. The quality that makes a work great.

He was pretty dejected and his year came to an end and he had to go back to work. Now he only had a couple of hours a day to work on a new book. And this one came a lot easier. It began to crackle with energy and at the end of the year he had sold it. Now it may be that the experience of completing a run-of-the-mill book had given him the literary muscle mass to write a better one, but equally it might be that dutifully slogging at his desk for eight hours a day meant that he produced an unexciting trudge of a book.

Key idea

Leonard Bernstein once said, 'To achieve great things, two things are needed; a plan, and not quite enough time', and I think this is true of writing novels. A little bit of panic helps concentrate the mind wonderfully.

People who can help

There is no getting around it: writing is a solitary pursuit. The only person wrestling with the blank page is you. Nigel Watts put it well when he said, 'The cauldron within which ideas bubble is not open for public inspection – it is just ourselves and the page.' You need to be detached from the world when you write. You need quiet contemplation, to allow your novel to find its own voice. I've said already in the course of this book that our novels are smarter than we are, because they are accessible to all of us – our unconscious as well as our everyday selves. And it's only in the silent wrestling with the dread force that is the blank white space of the screen or page that we allow our smart inner self to reach harbour.

However, other people can help and encourage, and provide midwifery for our project. It is for this reason that you should tell everyone that you are writing. Not only will your obvious seriousness help them to leave you space when you need it for the daily struggle, but once you've said that it is so, then you have made a start in making it so. You'll have to make it happen or risk calling your own bluff.

Other people can also provide practical help. They may tell you stories, give you research. If they care about you, they will want to help and you should listen because the stories they tell may be as good as they say, and they may fit the shape of your book. Or if not this one, then maybe the next one.

And then there are other writers. Writers rarely collaborate on novels (though it's not unknown – think of the pacey psychological thrillers of Nicci French, actually husband-and-wife team Sean French and Nicci Gerrard) but they do meet to share work and critique it and provide suggestions.

Writing groups and writers' circles

You may work alone, but ultimately you are not on your own. I said at the start of this chapter that writing is like a long-distance marathon. Only the individual runners need to actually run the required miles, but they still gather in clubs. And writers have their own equivalents of the local harriers.

Every town has its writing groups, though how open these are to new members varies hugely from group to group. Some are very informal, a group of friends meeting once a month to share new work and chat informally about writing. Others are more formal, led by a professional who teaches in an explicit fashion. My own group of around eight writers in West Yorkshire lasts for 90 minutes and in that time we produce two or three short pieces of writing from stimulus I give them. After each of these exercises, a couple will read back what they've done and we'll make brief comments before moving on to the next task. This is a writing group and is geared specifically towards the production of new work, which can be shaped and worked on by the group members in their own time.

My group takes place in the library and libraries are still the best place to find information about writing groups, writing circles, conferences, courses, readings and literature events. Librarians can often give impartial advice on what the activities are really like to help you decide whether it is for you.

You might need to experiment with going to a few writers' groups before finding one that suits your personality and way of working.

Writers' circles are different from writers' groups in that, rather than being about producing new work or about being taught how to write, they are instead about critiquing work written away from the group.

BLUEPRINT FOR A PERFECT WRITERS' CIRCLE

Some groups operate by allowing everyone the chance to read out work they've done over the preceding week or month or however long it is since the group last met. That just sounds like a recipe for word fatigue to me; no one can concentrate on being read to for that long, especially as the work is probably rough and unpolished. It also restricts the time for proper discussion or debate.

A good way for a writers' circle to operate is that each time the group meets for one or two 'stars of the week' (or month) to be chosen. They give the group an extract of, say, 2,000 words. The group reads and digests the extract, and at the next meeting the work is discussed – constructively and in detail. Crucially, the writer of the work must remain silent while the others dissect the extract. Only at the end of the allotted time should the author speak to clarify or defend their work.

It's hard to sit silently while your work is talked about by people who don't know the context or the background to the writing, and who may not know what's come before or what comes next. You may feel that they overlook words that have been hewn painfully from the unyielding rock strata of imagination, memory and observation, or that they haven't understood why a certain word was chosen in preference to another. But it's important to listen to readers talk in this way. And it is a privilege to have a committed group reading your work at an early stage. You can always dismiss what they say. You may very well be right, and they may be wrong, but if they are all saying similar things then it would be churlish not to give that some proper consideration. It's just as interesting, of course, if there is debate and argument about your work, with people holding radically opposing views. Again, it's completely up to you how you pick a path through the debate. Reject every one, if you want, but accept that it's a rare thing to have your work taken so seriously.

Another virtue of the writers' circle is that it makes you raise your game. You don't want to be found wanting in front of your peers. You'll check your work thoroughly before submitting it to their scrutiny. You'll read your manuscript through their eyes and make some changes accordingly. It'll make you bring some detachment to something you are emotionally very close to.

It's painful sometimes. Even constructive criticism can feel like a slap in the face to sensitive writers. Mild suggestions for improvement to writing you've laboured over can feel like a callous disregarding of all you've already done. But part of the point of a book like this is to desensitize you, to help you grow a second skin. A rhino-like hide is very useful in this game.

So it might sting, but best to keep your hurt and rage inside and then to read your manuscript again a day or two afterwards and see if, well, gosh, wouldn't you know it, some of those blighters have a point after all! No one will be too unnecessarily nasty. After all, they'll be submitting their work to you next, or in a few weeks' time.

Focus point

Remember, however, it is your book not theirs and you are master of this domain. Which is also something worth remembering when you come to start discussing your book with agents and editors. No matter how authoritative they might sound, it is YOU who are the real author. Always be ready to compromise, but be ready to stick to your guns when you have to. You are the expert when it comes to your book.

Snapshot

Have a quick Google to see if there are any writers' circles in your area. Try calling your local library or looking on Facebook. If there isn't one close enough, why not start your own?

Creative writing courses

EVENING CLASSES

Despite a recent move to emphasize very functional 'job skills'-type courses in evening classes, many authorities do still respond to popular demand and run creative writing classes. These may be similar to the groups and circles described, differing only in that they take place in a school hall rather than a meeting room, or in someone's house. They may also have a qualification attached to them. Again, your library is the place to find out about these. Websites for courses and master classes discussed here are given in Taking it further at the back of the book.

ARVON FOUNDATION COURSES AND RETREATS

I can whole-heartedly recommend these courses. The Arvon Foundation was set up in the late 1960s to provide retreats where writers can simply focus on their writing without distractions. There are four centres: the original centre, opened by poets John Moat and John Fairfax in Sheepwash, Devon; Lumb Bank in Ted Hughes' former home at Heptonstall in West Yorkshire; the Hurst in Shropshire (the former home of playwright John Osborne); and Moniack Mhor near Inverness in the Highlands.

All the houses are reasonably off the beaten track, simply furnished, and all cater for 16 emerging writers working closely with two established professionals. The courses last five days and typically consist of workshops in the mornings, one-to-one tutorials with the pros in the afternoon and readings in the evening. It sounds intensive, but it works. The group lives and works together for a week, even taking turns at cooking for each other.

There is something about the alchemy of being in a supportive community, away from the demands of work, spouses, children – away from the distractions of TV and the Internet – buried in the countryside. The tuition, the one-to-ones and the careful way the professional tutors read your work – all of this helps too, but it is the conversations with peers, plus the chance to think away from your usual environment, that make up the most valuable part of these courses.

I have been director of one of the Arvon centres, I have been a student on an Arvon course and I have been a tutor many times. I'm a fan. They really work. Wherever you are at with your novel when the week begins, you will be further ahead by the end of the week.

The Arvon Foundation is a charity dedicated to developing everyone's ability to write creatively. As a result they give grants to those who might otherwise struggle to pay the fees, and in fact it is the diversity of people attending that provides the real dynamism of an Arvon week. On Arvon courses I have met vicars and strippers, dukes and generals. I've met the man who set up the Iraqi health service under Saddam Hussein and I've met fountain designers and gardeners and students and ex-prisoners. On each course I've met people from all parts of the UK, but also from everywhere else too. And each course is a mix of men and women, upper, middle and working class, young and old, rural and urban. All united by the desire to produce the best book they can.

Further proof that an Arvon course works can be seen from the quality not just of the faculty, but also from the alumni. Booker Prize winner Pat Barker is an Arvon graduate, to give just one example, but there are lots of others.

Contact the Arvon Foundation at www.arvonfoundation.org.

TY NEWYDD

Ty Newydd is run on very similar lines to the Arvon Foundation and is based in Wales. The former home of David Lloyd George, Ty Newydd is on the coast in Criccieth and as well as providing week-long courses on the Arvon model, they also run some weekend courses. As the centre for new Welsh writing and supported by Literature Wales, they also run courses for those wishing to write in the Welsh language.

MASTER CLASSES

There are a lot of other organizations that have adapted the Arvon model. *The Guardian* newspaper, the publishers Faber and Faber and the agents Curtis Brown all run master classes where professional writers, and others involved in the industry, pass on their skills to aspiring writers for a fee (usually quite a substantial one). These can be very helpful for those with the necessary wedge to take advantage of them. They can give you information and practical help; what they can't give you is the camaraderie and peer-group support you get from a more immersive experience like Arvon.

Other publishers who run master classes include Tindal Street Press, Cinnamon Press and Peepal Tree Press.

There are also other retreats run by private individuals, often in sunnier places than the UK. In the US there are writers' colonies where food, accommodation and time to write are provided and writers gather in the evenings to talk and perhaps share work.

UNIVERSITY MA COURSES

I have an MA and what attracted me to my course at Manchester Metropolitan University was the fact that in order to qualify for the degree you had to actually complete your novel. Many universities simply require 40,000 words, which presumably means that there are lots of half-finished novels in the desk drawers of thousands of successful students. I also liked the fact that MMU allowed me to do the course part-time and to study by distance learning.

Distance learning meant my fellow students were based all over the world. My cohort contained students from Canada, Syria, Nigeria and Germany as well as from more glamorous spots such as Sidcup and Kettering. We used email and chat-room seminars and I don't think we lost anything by being an online group.

Doing the course part-time over a couple of years meant I could also keep my day job (working for the Arvon Foundation as it happened) and also spread the load of the fees.

What the course gave me was a reading list of contemporary novels, some of which I might not have discovered on my own. It also gave me feedback on my writing from highly regarded professors – all working novelists themselves – and, best of all, a supportive but competitive peer group, all of us committed to pushing each other along.

It isn't – and can't be – a guaranteed route to publication (I think from my year two of us were published within a year of the course finishing, though several others have in the five years since), but it can be a valuable form of propulsion. Certainly, I embarked on my novel thinking that if nothing else I would have a Master's degree and would have finished my book I'd been merely thinking of writing for the previous few years. Publication was, for me, an unexpected bonus.

Drawbacks to the course were having to write academic, critical essays of the kind I hadn't attempted since finishing my first degree nearly twenty years earlier, and having to do this when I just wanted to crack on with writing my own novel.

For many potential MA students a significant drawback will be the cost. I think the typical level of fee in the UK is about £5,000 per annum (pro-rata for part-time courses) and the general direction of travel is that these are set to rise steeply over the next few years. Some universities offer bursaries, however, and it is always worth investigating these.

DOCTORATES

And when you've finished your MA you might want to think about becoming a Doctor. Despite this meaning that people will be wanting to consult you about their bad knee or dodgy back at parties, studying for a doctorate in creative writing means you can teach writing in a university, and so perhaps support yourself while you write further novels. In order to get on to a PhD course, you will need to have a research project that will run alongside your novel. You will, in effect, be writing two books and both will have to meet stringent criteria before this advanced qualification is awarded.

PhDs usually run for three years and many universities offer a limited number of research fellowships where you are paid a small stipend while you write your novel and your research piece. In return you may be asked to do some teaching hours. These are usually advertised on www.jobs.ac.uk.

 Ernest Hemingway

'It's none of their business that you have to learn to write. Let them think you were born that way.'

Literary consultancies

Another development of the last ten years, a literary consultancy is an organization that will offer to critique part or all of your manuscript for a fee. Of these, the best known is TLC (standing for The Literary Consultancy, funnily enough), which is supported by Arts Council England and can, as a result, offer reductions and grants towards the cost for those who might struggle to pay.

When a writer sends in their manuscript to TLC, the consultancy arranges for a professional writer to compile a detailed report on it, pointing out strengths and weaknesses and making suggestions for improvement. It can be hard for new, raw-skinned writers to pay to read that their work is not up to the mark, but taking bad news on the chin and coming back stronger and hungrier than before is another thing that top athletes and the best writers share. You can't be afraid of someone's opinion. And it is just an opinion. It always remains your book, yours to change or not as you see fit.

TLC is the best known, but there are others including (see the Resources section at the back of the book):

- Annette Green Agency
- Cornerstones.

Writing agencies

A number of agencies exist to help new writers by providing a mixture of mentoring, live readings, discussions, workshops and platform opportunities. These are generally regionally based and, like TLC, supported by Arts Council England, Creative Scotland, and Arts Council of Northern Ireland. In the age of Google, writers can pick and choose a range of support from several agencies and are not simply restricted to the one they live nearest to. Many of the programmes are available to anyone with a PC.

The key writing agencies are:

- Spread The Word (London)
- New Writing North (based in Newcastle)
- Literature North-West (based in Manchester)

- Commonword (based in Manchester)
- Writing West Midlands (based in Birmingham)
- Writing East Midlands (based in Nottingham)
- Cypress Well (based in Exeter)
- New Writing South (based in Southampton)
- Writer's Centre (based in Norwich)
- Literature Wales.

Details for these can be in found in the Resources section at the back of the book. Again, as publicly funded organizations these agencies may be able to help sponsor you in getting some of the practical support you need, as well as providing support networks of other writers in your area.

Festivals and conferences

There are many literary festivals and several writers' conferences and it can be very helpful for those writing a novel to attend. Several will run workshops for writers led by professionals, and others will offer you the chance to pitch your ideas or work to agents. Among the best, either because they have a lot of events or because I know that they are very well run, are:

- Hay Festival
- Cheltenham Literature Festival
- Ilkley Literature Festival
- Edinburgh Book Festival
- Manchester Literature Festival
- Hebden Bridge Arts Festival
- Durham Book Festival
- Harrogate Crime Writing Festival
- Birmingham Book Festival
- Winchester Writers' Conference
- York Festival of Ideas.

Websites for those listed above can be found in the Resources section at the end of the book. In addition to this, the British Council maintains a list of all the literature festivals taking place over the year and you can usually also find details in the *Writers' and Artists' Yearbook* (A & C Black), which, if you are serious about writing a novel and getting it published, is a must-have.

In terms of support, this is a very good time to be a writer. There has never been such a good time to build networks that can cajole, encourage, coax and harass your book out of you.

Next step

In this chapter we have seen that a chair, a flat surface and a pen are all you need to write. It is the most democratic of art forms. You should, however, make time for your writing; don't just wait for it to materialize. Skill comes with practice, so write regularly. We've also seen that there are many places where you can find help, support and inspiration, from the Internet to local writers' groups. In the next chapter, we'll be moving on to look at what happens when your novel is finished and ready to go out into the world.

14

Marketing your manuscript

Here's an important piece of advice: finish your book before you send it out. And by finish, I mean really finish. I mean a complete polished draft from 'Once upon a time...' to '...happily ever after' (or however your book starts and ends). It should be a story that has gone through the full distillation process, a novel that has been drafted, left to compost, taken out, read aloud, redrafted, sent to critical, candid, but constructive friends – and then redrafted again, left again, redrafted again, honed, tweaked, buffed and copy-edited until you are absolutely certain that you can't do any more to it. Do not send any parts of your book to agents or publishers until you've finished it. Don't use these people to get validation. They are not the people for that – that's what your friends or your writing group are for. Agents, editors – they are just people, but they are busy people and you don't want to be wasting their time.

Unless you are very famous (and you're not, are you?) or unless you already have a track record as a novelist (and you don't, do you?), then any agent or publisher is simply going to nod and smile and say 'Sounds good, send it to me when you've finished.'

Focus point

Don't use agents for self-validation. Make sure the book is as polished as possible before sending it out.

Agents

A question that new writers often ask is whether they should go to an agent or approach a publisher directly. These days that is very simple. If you want to be published by a mainstream publisher, then you will need to go through an agent. Publishers use agents as a filtering system, and you can't blame them. It is said that there are a million manuscripts in the offices of agents and publishers in London, all looking for a home. And who has time to read all that?

Agents want to make money and so it is their job to know the marketplace, to know what is likely to sell. They also build up relationships with publishers and get to know their tastes too. A good agent will know what individual editors are looking for, and also the direction the market as a whole is moving in. If you are looking to make money from your novel, especially if you are looking for money upfront – the advance – then you will need an agent to represent you.

There aren't very many big publishers – maybe six really big ones who have multiple imprints – and then there another handful of what you might call major independents (e.g. Faber, Bloomsbury). These are the companies who will pay an advance (money up front against future sales). Then there is another world of smaller independents most of whom pay tiny or no advances. And then there are the many tiny independent publishers – many of them with only one editor/owner who works from his or her kitchen table – putting out a handful of titles a year. Many of these are very good (see later in the chapter), but you don't usually need an agent for these.

An agent will act as a broker between you and the best publisher for your work. If they take you on, they will work with you on tightening the book one more time (because yes, there is always more editing and redrafting to do). Remember the mantra: all writing is rewriting. Your agent will then champion your book and pitch it, and if they are trusted agents, the publishers will listen. They might not go for your book in the end, but they will at least consider it carefully. If you are represented by an agent with a track record for discovering great books, then an editor would be mad not to read your book.

Once an agent has found a publisher that is interested, then the fun can really begin. You only need one publisher of course, but things can get really exciting if several want your book. Then it is up for auction and – like any other auction – the winner is usually the one that pays more than any of the others think it's worth, which can often have drawbacks down the line. For this reason, agents may steer their writers away from just accepting the best offer. They may want you to consider your personal chemistry with the editor, the publisher's own track record in marketing new writers, what rights will be sold and what you'll be able to hang on to. It can be a complicated business and an experienced agent is your guide through it.

The relationship a writer will have with an agent will vary. Some do a lot of editing before sending the book out, working very closely with the author. Some become friends and are on call to provide sympathy, reassurance and warmth whenever the authors need it. Others are very much more distant, confining their conversations strictly to business. As you would expect, most are on the spectrum between the two points. It is worth bearing in mind that, as with any relationship that involves money, you will almost certainly never be quite friends. One agent I know reckoned she had to lose the lowest-earning 15 per cent of her list every year, in order to have time to take on new authors. That kind of focus is always going to break some hearts.

The bottom line is you want an agent because you hope they'll make you money; a certain degree of ruthlessness is what they get their percentage for. I have one writer friend who loves his agent because he describes her as an 'absolute Rottweiler'. He himself is big and soft and kind and fluffy and would also agree to anything a publisher suggested. He would write his books for nothing probably, and so having an attack dog looking out for him makes good sense. I'm not like that. I'm uncomfortable around dogs, even tiny yappy ones, never mind weapon dogs. So it's important for me to have an agent I can talk to. Someone who shares at least some of my tastes and who is tolerant of psychological frailties and is amiable and easy to be around. (I do still hope he kicks butt when it matters though.) Of course it is tough to get a decent agent – we don't always get a choice – but you can make that process a little easier for yourself.

Key idea

If you want a contract with a big publisher, you will almost certainly need an agent.

Augusten Burroughs

'As a writer, you can't allow yourself the luxury of being discouraged and giving up when you are rejected, either by agents or publishers. You absolutely must plow forward.'

GETTING AN AGENT

Let's be clear about one thing. There is no secret code to getting an agent. There's no special handshake, no magic words. There's no one you can meet who has a special route in. It's not like smuggling diamonds or weapons; you don't need a fixer. There's no party to go to where you might meet the person with a golden key. There is no golden key.

And despite what you sometimes might feel, it doesn't really matter how old you are or what you look like. It does help if you are well known in another field already. And if that field is television or journalism, then that helps too. But it is still about the actual work in the end. It is a kind of cliché but still worth repeating: in my experience if you stumble across a gathering of agents then they might very well be talking about books and literature, while a similar gathering of novelists will be talking about money.

HOW TO PRESENT YOUR MANUSCRIPT

At one level, all you need to do to get an agent is finish your book, and put the first three chapters in an envelope with a 250-word synopsis. You need to make sure the pages are 1.5 or double-spaced and printed on one side of the paper only. If you want feedback, include a stamped addressed envelope (this doesn't mean you'll necessarily get any, but it makes it a lot more likely).

These are general rules, but make sure you check with the agent's website for any specific requirements that the agency has. The

Writers' and Artists' Yearbook also contains information on how to contact agents, including what sort of material they deal with. It is pointless to send your historical epic to an agency that only deals in children's literature.

Focus point

Invest in a copy of the latest *Writers' and Artists' Yearbook*.

Beyond these general rules, there are things you can do to ensure that your book stands more of a chance than the other 999,999 manuscripts.

Always send your manuscript to a named agent. If you just send it to the agency, the chances are it will be read by the intern or the receptionist. They may love it enough to insist that a proper agent reads it, but they might not. This book has taken you years to write, you want to make sure the best person reads it, don't you? You want to give it its best shot.

Do your homework – first-time novelists always thank their agent in the acknowledgements. Find out who represents authors whose works you admire. It also makes sense to send your work to those who represent writers who seem to be operating in the same area as you, or writers whose style shares some similarities with yours. There is at least a likelihood then that your tastes may coincide, or that what attracted the agent to those writers may also attract him or her to you.

Do some more homework – find out, if you can, who in the agency is actively looking for new writers. When an agent says their list is full, they probably mean it. What you want is someone who has perhaps joined the agency quite recently, or someone who has just made the transition from assistant or associate to full agent. The receptionist may be the best person to furnish you with this sort of information.

Write a good covering letter – and by good I mean short and to the point. Tell your reader what the book is about briefly. Tell them you've heard they're a good agent (a little judicious flattery can't hurt, as long as it is subtly and believably done). Let them know you've come to them because they represent x or y whose books you much admire.

Mention any prizes you've won, any writing qualifications you have (though don't expect your MA to magically open any doors). Don't say a lot about your job, unless it's a particularly unusual one or if it informs the novel in some way. (Fountain designer good; English teacher probably not so good, unless your book is that elusive thing – a brilliant novel set in a high school.)

Make sure your pages and your letter are pristine, thoroughly spell-checked and proofread and sent in a proper jiffy bag. What you don't want is something sent in an envelope that explodes in a cloud of grey chaff when your potential agent opens it, ruining her outfit. It will just mean that she hates your book before she's read a word.

Agents will tell you not to approach more than one at a time. I don't really agree with this. Send copies of your manuscript out in batches and if one calls offering a meeting, you can ring the others and see if they have read your work too. Don't ring before this point, however. There's no point hassling or nagging. Agents will read your work. It might take them a while, but they will in the end. Of course they will. The whole industry depends upon the finding and nurturing of new talent and no one wants to be Dick Rowe. Have you not heard of Dick Rowe? He was the man who in 1962 turned down The Beatles for Decca because 'groups with guitars are on the way out'. In 1962! When groups with guitars had only just got started. Similarly, there are plenty of agents still blushing at odd moments, whenever it comes back to them that they once rejected a charming but slight story of trainee wizards by a young writer called Joanne.

THE SYNOPSIS

I tend to think that a flexible synopsis is more use to a writer than to an agent. You need to know where you're going as you write the book – though as the god of the novel's universe you can change the story as you go if a better idea comes along. No one should be the slave to their synopsis. However, all agents now request a synopsis and I'm baffled by this. Surely if they like your first three chapters then they'll read the rest? And if they don't like those chapters then the fact the plot is intricately worked out surely doesn't matter much.

Nevertheless, a synopsis is what seems to be required. So make it tight and focused. Give it personality, so show a flavour of your writing. Make sure the contrasts between characters and their conflicts come over clearly, but above all make sure the story is clear. That's what the synopsis is really for – to give your prospective agent the sense that there are twists and surprise in this book. That stuff actually happens. Far too many novelists think that 100,000 words of beautiful prose is a novel. It really isn't. At some level all books have to be thrillers. Literary ones, complicated ones, psychological ones, romantic ones or comical ones – but there has to be some propulsion behind them. Something to keep the reader turning the page.

Snapshot

Practise writing synopses. Write them for your favourite books, write them for films, write them for your own work. Keep practising until it feels natural.

Focus point

Most agents will want a synopsis – make sure this is short and focused on the story.

It is true that the law of supply and demand means the odds are definitely stacked against you when it comes to getting an agent. In the writing game there is always a lot of supply and little demand – especially for debut authors. However, the odds are not quite as bleak as they first appear. Of those million manuscripts in the offices of agents and publishers, 90 per cent won't be any good and half of the others will be badly presented, or will have been sent to the wrong person. That still leaves 50,000 so those are still long odds, but you have given yourself an extra edge by reading this book (and maybe even some others like it) and, also, you know it can be done. I've done it. Lots of other people have. You can do it too.

Key idea

Agents will read your work. No one wants to miss out on the next J. K. Rowling.

Independent publishers – the 'small presses'

There has been a huge upheaval in the publishing industry. Over the last 20 years many of the long established houses have been taken over by big multinationals who do many other things besides publish books. They produce films, DVDs, music, newspapers, electronic communications, games, downloads. The names of the publishers may survive, but they tend to be imprints within these giant corporations. This means there are fewer editors, paying less for books. Where the publishing imprints are fighting for survival, trying to prove to accountants who run the businesses that they are a contributor to profits rather than a drain on company resources, then editors are going to have a balance sheet in mind when they think about offering for a book.

Editors will still want to grow an author. They will still take risks. But they maybe won't give an author quite so long to develop a career, and the risks will be more calculated. Arguably the biggest result of this kind of rationalization has been that mainstream publishing is more homogenous than ever before. If editors are looking for possible high-volume sales from each title, then they will, it is claimed, stick to what they already know sells.

I'm not sure about this. My experience is that in publishing – as in any other industry – playing it safe is actually suicide. Following the herd just means you tumble off the cliff after the other lemmings, and smart editors know this. When the market is in freefall, that's when to invest.

However, there is no doubt that it is harder than it's ever been to get a big commercial publisher behind you, even if you have a good and powerful agent. Fortunately changes in printing technology and the general advance of digital technology have meant that the number and quality of smaller indie publishers – the 'small presses' – has grown. This means that even if you fail to secure an agent then you can still find someone who can get your book out to the marketplace.

Most of the indie presses will take submissions from those who are not represented by agents. It is worth researching them properly (again, the *Writers' and Artists' Yearbook* will list them and provide basic details about them). There are huge differences between the independents. Differences in size, finance, number of books published per year, quality and impact. Look at websites, but also try to see if you can find books published by them in the shops. See if their books are reviewed in the press. Read a selection of their books to see if you like the range and quality of the product. And, if you do decide to submit direct to these publishers, take the same care as you would over a letter to one of the major publishers. I would follow the same rules you did when submitting to agents too.

Many of the indies were set up by one or two passionate individuals and so have a very clear vision about the kind of books they want to publish. And the fact that they very often have a heavy personal financial stake in the business means that authors get special care and attention from the editor. It may also mean that writers get more creative control than they would from a major who has shareholders to satisfy.

Many writers who sign with small presses talk about feeling part of a family, rather than a cog in a machine. Several indies have had successes with prizes and surprise bestsellers, and even where they haven't broken an artist through to the mainstream, they have acted as a nursery where talent can grow and develop even if in the end the writer breaks through to wider public consciousness with a more commercial publisher.

It is worth saying too that some smaller presses get public support from Arts Council England (or their equivalents in other territories), which insulates them at least a little from commercial pressures, allowing them to pursue a more idiosyncratic experimental path than other editorial directors would get away with.

Digital publishing

Digital publishing has also levelled the playing field between majors and smaller presses to a certain extent. Once upon a time a major could simply afford to press more copies of a book than less financially muscular competitors. With the rise of Kindle and other e-readers, scarcity in books has been abolished. You don't need a printer, a warehouse, a distribution network and shops in order to sell books. Many of the barriers to entry to the marketplace for publishing entrepreneurs have simply vanished.

There is no limit to the number of copies of a book that can be downloaded, so when it comes to digital versions of books the smaller publisher can get as many virtual books on to a reader's virtual shelves as anyone else. Similarly, expensive cover art is not an issue with ebooks.

There are a large number of publishers who now only publish ebooks. This is not what most authors want. Most writers still prize a physical product. Interestingly, younger writers in particular prize print – this is possibly because they have been brought up as digital natives, well aware that anything can be posted up on the Internet regardless of merit. However, if someone has invested time in choosing typefaces and cover art and taking it to a printer and warehousing it and distributing it in a physical form, well that means it's something rare and special.

Nevertheless, digital publishing does render the book marketplace a more democratic forum; there are far more places to put your work and e-publishing shouldn't be dismissed. Many authors self-publish their work digitally first and can – through cannily low pricing on Amazon and similar places – build a following. Some stories and novels are free to download, even by established names. These are seen as loss leaders, ways to build an audience that might pay for material later down the line.

The biggest publishing phenomenon of recent times, E. L. James's *50 Shades of Grey* (Vintage Books, 2011) famously began life as fan fiction on a website for fans of Stephanie Meyer's Twilight series (Little, Brown, 2005–8), before being bought and rebooted by mainstream publishers.

Snapshot

Have a look at the best-selling ebooks on Amazon. Could you see your novel there?

Self-publishing

This is not vanity publishing. Vanity publishing is where a company offers to become your publisher for a fee. They will undertake to edit, design, print and distribute your book and you will pay them. This is an expensive way to put out a book, and the services provided by these companies are variable.

Self-publishing is where you are the publisher and you control these processes. You will still be taking on the risk and there will still be considerable costs. But advances in technology, particularly in the area of print-on-demand, means it is more affordable than it ever has been.

I wouldn't ever do it myself. I need to know that my book has passed some external quality control. I am not so confident in my own critical faculties that I think I can curb my own excesses. It is the fact that other people are willing to place their trust and – crucially – their own money in backing my work that gives me what faith I have in my own talent.

But others take a different view. Timothy Mo – a multiple award-winner writer of literary fiction – self-publishes, and others self-publish at least some of their work. The thinking is, why should a publisher take the majority of the profits of a book, when the author can do so much of this for themselves?

Writers who take this route are choosing to brand themselves as Independent Authors, drawing an explicit link with indie publishers and indie bookshops. They are offering something outside the mainstream but in a professional and business-like way, and creating more choice in a market that might otherwise be dominated by a handful of the same old faces.

If you are going to do it properly, you should think about the following:

- Get your work critiqued by a creditable editorial consultancy and act on their suggestions.
- Work closely with a freelance editor. There are a lot of people about doing this work, many of them former employees of major publishing houses or still working for major publishers on a freelance basis.
- Hire a good graphic designer and a good printer used to working with books. Shop around. Talk to people, and join organizations and networks which will provide support and advice. Go to seminars organized at writers' conferences and literary festivals (see Chapter 13).

- When you are absolutely your text is exactly how you want it, and when the book has been copy-edited and proofread multiple times, only then can you consider getting it printed.
- On top of all this, you'll need an ISBN to get the book signed up to Amazon and other online retailers. You'll need to be prepared to spend a lot of time promoting your book through social media such as Twitter and Facebook, or hire an agency to do that for you.
- Don't expect to get your novel into shops, other than in your local area, easily. The big chains – e.g. Waterstones and Barnes & Noble – increasingly make buying decisions centrally and have restricted the range of titles from debut authors that they stock.

One of the things that makes self-publishing easier for writers now is that there are many networks where authors come together to share information, advice and help. There a number of these networks, both formal and informal – and, in an interesting development, the old established literary agency of A. M. Heath is contractually linked to one of these in order to represent independent writers.

So, yes, self-publishing is an option. For the more entrepreneurial of authors it might even be fun. Most writers these days are smart and business-savvy. They have to be, and readers can be reached directly through blogs and social networks so that news about a great new novel can spread much faster than ever before.

Digital publishing means you will never run out of stock and can compete on a level playing field with the big boys in the ebook department at least. If it goes well, the bigger publishers will be queuing up to sign your book anyway, so it can be a way of getting noticed. But, a note of caution, only go down this route if you think you have the editorial, business and marketing skills to go with your fiction writing talent.

 Edna St. Vincent Millay

'A person who publishes a book willfully appears before the populace with his pants down. If it is a good book nothing can hurt him. If it is a bad book nothing can help him.'

Workshop

If you think self-publishing is the way to go, ask yourself the following questions:

- Is your book absolutely finished? Has it been checked, checked and checked again, read by trusted and intelligent friends, maybe professionally edited and basically polished to a high gleam? If not, stop. You are not ready.
- Are you social media-savvy? A huge part of self-publishing is marketing. Many self-published writers have busy blogs and Facebook pages and are very active on Twitter. If this sort of thing gives you the heebie-jeebies, self-publishing might not be for you.
- Do you read self-published fiction yourself? Do you know your target audience? Who else is self-publishing in your genre or style? If you are going to enter the world of self-publishing, it would be rude – and unwise – not to read the work of your 'colleagues'.
- Have you researched the boring, technical side of things, like formatting and authors' rights? You need to make sure you know what you are doing, because there is no one else to blame if things go wrong.

All this might sound a bit off-putting, but remember that you're not alone. There are hundreds of success stories and thousands of websites offering self-publishing advice. There's a community waiting for you out there in the ether.

HELP AND ADVICE FOR SELF-PUBLISHERS

The following organizations may be of use to anyone considering self-publishing:

- Alliance of Independent Authors: www.allianceindependentauthors.org
- Independent Authors Guild: www.independentauthorsguild.com
- Coalition of Independent Authors: www.coalition-independent-authors.com

- Independent Author Network:
  www.independentauthornetwork.com
- Smashwords: www.smashwords.com
- Lulu Publishing: www.lulu.com

The nations and the regions

Many independent publishers are also based in the regions. I know many writers (and readers too!) are unhappy at the idea that all serious publishing must take place in London or New York. Books with a strong regional identity or market might easily be overlooked by metropolitan publishing houses looking for global sales. This means that these writers often find a place in publishers based closer to home, who understand the context in which they were written.

It may be that for one or all these reasons you feel that your novel will fit better with a smaller independent than with a traditional, mainstream imprint. It is worth pointing out that most small presses will offer only very small advances – if at all – though some will pay an enhanced royalty rate to compensate.

Snapshot

Do an Internet search for independent presses in your region. Have a look at their websites. Buy some of their books. It's always worth supporting local publishers and writers.

What do I want from my book?

Snapshot

Try the following: make a list of all the things you want from publishing your book. Be honest: if fame or money is important, put that down too. If it's creative control you're after, put that down. Assign each item you note down a mark out of five. This should help you determine where to send your manuscript: to an agent, or to an independent publisher.

How much will I get for my book?

Most first-time novelists with a major publisher will get a small advance against royalties, meant to pay for living expenses while they work on their book. These may vary from as little as a few thousand pounds to several hundred thousand pounds depending on the nature of the deal. Advances do not usually have to be repaid if the book fails to recoup the money spent on it.

From a strictly financial point of view, the best thing that can happen to a new novelist is if their book goes to auction. This means that several publishers are keen to have the rights to the book, and will bid against each other to make sure they get to put the book out.

Of course there are other things to consider if your book goes to auction. It is not simply about the money. You might want to think about your chemistry with the editor. Will you be able to get along when you work with each other closely? Do you trust one another? What about the rest of the company? Do they have the personnel, track record, marketing plan and financial muscle to be able to do their best with the book? All of these are considerations which need to be borne in mind when deciding which of the many suitors for your book should be taken seriously.

Agents like to sell the rights for a book to one country at a time. They will hope to sell the book to the UK for one amount and possibly sign the book to another publisher in the US. They will also hope to retain translation rights for an author, as well as rights for film and television adaptations.

Publishers, on the other hand will want to negotiate World Rights, meaning that when they buy the rights they buy them for publication in all territories. They may also want to tie the author to a two-book deal. This means they not only buy the finished book, but also another book as yet unwritten. They buy one completed book, and your idea for the next book. It can sound mad: after all the struggle and sweat of writing (and rewriting one book), finding an agent, redrafting again, then finding editors who are interested and then discovering that your next book is a sought after property without so much as one word being written! Nevertheless, that's often how it works.

A typical deal

In many ways there are no typical deals, especially with the book market in such revolutionary flux as it is at the moment. Here is one fairly midscale deal.

World rights for two books.

The author is paid an advance of £25,000 in five stages:

- 25% on signing the contract
- 25% on first publication
- 25% upon delivery of book 2
- 12.5% upon first publication of book 2
- 12.5% upon paperback publication of book 2.

There is likely to be at least a year's gap between signing and the first publication of this author's book. Plus the agent will take 15 per cent of the fee as commission on which (in the UK) 20-per-cent VAT is payable. The author must then pay tax on the remainder of his advance, so you can see this author is not getting rich any time soon. And his advance is by no means negligible. Compared to many offered these days, it's not bad at all.

This author does get 10 per cent of the retail price in royalties on books sold (again, subject to 15-per-cent commission), but only once the whole advance is paid back. So the advance for the second book has to be repaid along with the first, before this writer gets any more money from the publishers.

So, you can see that most novelists are unlikely to get rich and, in fact, when you add up all the time you've spent on your novel, you have almost certainly been working for less than the national wage.

Again, you see why authors might be attracted to self-publishing online where they would typically get nearly all of the purchase price of the book even if that is very low. Sell 20,000 copies of a £10 book and the average mainstream author gets £20,000 in royalties. Sell 100,000 copies of your self-published ebook at 20p a copy and you also make £20,000.

Of course, despite what you read in the press very few self-published authors sell anything like 100,000 copies of their books. And, with no marketing support, they might struggle to sell 1 per cent of this number, even at a penny a book.

Key idea

Very few people have ever got rich from writing. Those who have aren't the best writers.

Stephen King

'Writing isn't about making money, getting famous, getting dates, getting laid, or making friends. In the end, it's about enriching the lives of those who will read your work, and enriching your own life, as well. It's about getting up, getting well, and getting over. Getting happy, okay? Getting happy.'

Next step

In this chapter we've looked at the ways in which you can get your book out there, into the welcoming arms of the reading public. By now you have studied every aspect of how to write your novel, the one only you can write, and hopefully you have managed to produce a piece of work you are proud of.

In the next section you will find resources that will help you to take your career as a writer further, developing your skills and networks and making writing a central part of your life.

Resources

The following list is not exhaustive, but just a snapshot of what is available for writers. There are supportive communities out there, and they probably meet in your library. (And if they don't, your librarian knows how to find them – every writer should make sure they are intimately acquainted with their library.)

Research

projectbritain.com – contains lots of information on calendar dates, folklore, customs, etc.

www.academicindex.net – research website.

www.opsi.gov.uk – resource site which includes information on the Freedom of Information Act.

www.bl.uk – British Library site which includes newspaper archives

dictionary.reference.com – an American site which includes dictionary and thesaurus.

www.infoplease.com – a huge site including dictionary, atlas, encyclopaedia and almanacs.

www.snopes.com – online hoax-buster. Great for ascertaining the veracity of the countless weird stories that circulate online and that a writer might be tempted to steal.

www.writerswrite.com/reference – a long list of links to sites containing everything from baby names to crime stories. Something for everyone.

Support

www.jbwb.co.uk – a British site which gives information on markets, competitions and agents; offers a critique and editing service for all forms of writing.

www.firstwriter.com – UK resource site covering literary agents, book publishers, writing competitions and magazines, from all over the English-speaking world.

www.writewords.org.uk – a British database site offering feedback to writers, support, advice, opportunities, competitions and news; subscription required.

Opportunities

www.authonomy.com – HarperCollins website where writers can upload their novels for free.

www.wattpad.com – Read or create stories for free. A vast site that has seen several of its writers go on to mainstream success. Quite heavy on the fanfiction though.

www.writeon.amazon.com – Amazon's answer to Wattpad – a site that enables you to write, read and review stories.

www.booktrust.org.uk – A great site that includes a list of UK writing competitions.

Writers' organizations

www.alcs.co.uk – the Authors' Licensing and Collecting Society is able to remunerate authors with secondary royalties via collective licensing schemes from photocopying, etc.

www.plr.uk.com – administered by Public Lending Right based in Stockton-upon-Tees and funded by the Department for Culture, Media and Sport (DCMS).

www.societyofauthors.org – The Society of Authors is a trade union for professional authors, dealing with financial and legal problems which they might encounter.

Writing agencies

These are publically subsidized organizations set up to help and support writers and develop literature. They work in different ways, but generally they all provide mentoring, workshops and platform opportunities. They also provide networks that connect individual writers and writers' groups in a region. The following are the major ones:

Spread The Word (London): www.spreadtheword.org.uk

New Writing North (Northern England): www.newwritingnorth.com

Literature North-West: www.literaturenorthwest.co.uk

Commonword (Manchester and North-West): www.cultureword.org.uk

Writing West Midlands: www.writingwestmidlands.org

Writing East Midlands: www.writingeastmidlands.co.uk

Writer's Centre Norwich: www.writerscentrenorwich.org.uk

New Writing South: www.newwritingsouth.com

Literature Wales: www.literaturewales.org

Writer's Federation (Scotland): writersfederation.org.uk

Courses

There are a huge number of courses that have sprung up to support writers. There are nearly a hundred university MA courses to choose from and an increasing number of undergraduate courses too. (The nearest university to you probably runs one.) In addition to these, agents, publishers and even writers offer master classes. Here are some of the best:

The Arvon Foundation: Provides five-day residential courses, taught by professional writers in three large houses with literary connections – www.arvonfoundation.org

Ty Newydd: The Welsh equivalent of the Arvon Foundation based in Lloyd George's old house in Criccieth, West Wales – www.tynewydd.org

Faber Academy: This established independent publisher runs residential courses in selected cities across the world – www.faberacademy.co.uk

Guardian Masterclasses: *The Guardian* newspaper organizes master classes in all aspects of writing (including self-publishing) – www.guardian.co.uk/guardian-masterclasses

Curtis Brown Creative: Curtis Brown are one of the biggest literary agencies and have recently set up courses where writers they represent – as well as their agents – teach how to write, present and pitch novels so that you have the best chance of success – www.curtisbrowncreative.co.uk

Tindal Street Press: Known for encouraging new writers – www.tindalstreet.co.uk

Cinnamon Press: Offers a range of writing awards and competitions to help writers establish a writing profile – www.cinnamonpress.com

Peepal Tree Press: Focuses on the best in Caribbean and Black British fiction, poetry, literary criticism, memoirs and historical studies – www.peepaltreepress.com

Literary consultancies

These are organizations who will critique your manuscript (for a fee). Those listed here are some of the best known and/or most reliable. They use experienced professional writers to write reports on the work submitted.

The Literary Consultancy: www.literaryconsultancy.co.uk

Cornerstones: www.cornerstones.co.uk

Oxford Literary Consultancy: http://www.oxfordwriters.com/

Annette Green Agency: www.annettegreenagency.co.uk

A.M. Heath: www.amheath.com

Festivals and conferences

There are thousands of writing festivals, but the ones listed here also offer courses, mentoring and the chance to get help and advice from authors, agents and publishers.

Birmingham Book Festival: www.birminghambookfestival.org

Cheltenham Literature Festival: www.cheltenhamfestivals.com/literature

Durham Book Festival: www.durhambookfestival.com

Edinburgh Book Festival: www.edbookfest.co.uk

Harrogate Crime Writing Festival: www.harrogateinteranationalfestivals.com/crime

Harrogate International Crime Writing Festival: harrogateinternationalfestivals.com/crime

Hay Festival: www.hayfestival.com

Hebden Bridge Arts Festival: www.hebdenbridge.co.uk/festival

Ilkley Literature Festival: www.ilkleyliteraturefestival.org.uk

Manchester Literature Festival: www.manchesterliteraturefestival. co.uk

Winchester Writers' Conference: www.writersconference.co.uk

York Festival of ideas: yorkfestivalofideas.com

Recommended reading

Aristotle, *On the Art of Poetry*, published as *Classical Literary Criticism* (Penguin Classics, 1965). Literary theory stripped to the bone. Essential reading, if only to disagree with it.

Armstrong, David, *How Not to Write a Novel: Confessions of a Midlist Author* (Allison & Busby Limited, 2003). Warm, witty and generous advice from a man who knows that you won't be talked out of writing your book, no matter how hard he tries.

Allott, Miriam, *Novelists on the Novel* (Routledge and Kegan Paul, 1959). A compendium of quotations from novelists about all aspects of novel writing. Out of print now, but worth tracking a copy down.

Boylan, Clare (ed.), *The Agony and the Ego* (Penguin Books, 1993). Essays by contemporary fiction writers.

Braine, John, *Writing a Novel* (Methuen, 1974). Author of *Room at the Top*. Stern and authoritative advice based on years of experience.

Brande, Dorothea, *Becoming a Writer* (Macmillan, 1996). Perhaps the most loved book on creative writing. First published in 1934, its inspirational and insightful message is still going strong. Valuable writing exercises to get you started – foreword by Malcolm Bradbury.

Cappacchione, Lucia, *The Power of the Other Hand* (Newcastle, 1988). 'Clustering' exercises as a way into your store of inspiration.

Casterton, Julia, *Creative Writing* (Macmillan, 1986). Practical, intelligent and humane.

Doubtfire, Dianne, *The Craft of Novel-Writing* (Allison and Busby, 1978). *Creative Writing* (Hodder and Stoughton, 1996). Thorough, no-nonsense advice with plenty of examples from texts.

Fairfax, John, *Creative Writing* (Elm Tree Books, 1989).

Fairfax, John, with John Moat, *The Way to Write* (Elm Tree Books, 1981). The founders of the Arvon Foundation: both experienced poets. Useful exercises.

Forster, E. M., *Aspects of the Novel* (Pelican Books, 1962). A collection of lectures delivered at Cambridge University in 1927. Fresh and unaffected, this book has become a classic. Invaluable chapters on plot and character.

Goldberg, Natalie, *Writing Down the Bones* (Shambala, 1986). *Wild Mind* (Bantam, 1990). A Zen poetess and teacher of creative writing. The most inspirational writer on the subject that I know.

King, Stephen, *On Writing* (Hodder & Stoughton, 2000). He's got a bit of a track record in this writing lark.

Kitchen, Paddy, *The Way to Write Novels* (Elm Tree Books, 1981). Another Arvon tutor: a personal and approachable style.

Klauser, Henriette Anne *Writing on Both Sides of the Brain* (Harper & Row, 1986). Exercises on free thinking techniques.

Lodge, David, *The Art of Fiction* (Penguin Books, 1992). A fascinating collection of articles from *The Independent on Sunday*, useful for the reader as well as the writer.

Paris Review Interviews *Writers at Work* (7 vols) (Secker & Warburg and Penguin, 1958–85). An invaluable insight into the minds and working methods of successful writers.

Shaugnessy, Susan, *Meditations for Writers* (HarperCollins, 1993). Affirmations and helpful quotes to keep you going.

Strunk, William, and E. B. White, *The Elements of Style* (Macmillan, 1979). The book on style by two masters.

Thomas, Scarlett, *Monkeys With Typewriters* (Canongate Books Ltd, 2012). Thomas has published nine novels and teaches creative writing at Kent University. A distinctive take on what it means to fictionalize your life.

Ueland, Brenda, *If You Want to Write* (Element Books, 1991). First published in 1938. Delightful and inspiring.

Wilson, Colin, *The Craft of the Novel* (Gollancz, 1975). An interesting history of the development of the craft of the novel.

Reference books

Wells, Gordon, *The Book Writer's Handbook* (Allison and Busby, 1989).

Allen, R. E., *The Oxford Writer's Dictionary* (Oxford University Press, 1990). Invaluable for those tricky questions of style and usage.

The Writer's Handbook (Papermac, published yearly). Almost every address you would ever need.

Writers' and Artists' Yearbook (A & C Black, published yearly). Much the same as the above. Useful chapters on finances, the law, publishing practices, etc.

Whitaker's Books in Print™ to see if anyone has got there before you.

Magazines for writers

Writers' News and Writing Magazine – UK based: www.writers-online.co.uk/Writing-Magazine/

Writers' Forum – UK based: www.writers-forum.com

Writer's Digest – US based: www.writersdigest.com

Mslexia – UK based, for women who write: www.mslexia.co.uk

Index